The New Testament as Literature:
A Very Short Introduction

Purchased by the
Memorial-
Endowment Fund

Very Short Introductions available now:

PSYCHOLOGY Gillian Butler and
    Freda McManus
THE QUAKERS Pink Dandelion
QUANTUM THEORY
    John Polkinghorne
RACISM Ali Rattansi
RELIGION IN AMERICA
    Timothy Beal
THE RENAISSANCE Jerry Brotton
RENAISSANCE ART
    Geraldine A. Johnson
ROMAN BRITAIN Peter Salway
THE ROMAN EMPIRE
    Christopher Kelly
ROUSSEAU Robert Wokler
RUSSELL A. C. Grayling
RUSSIAN LITERATURE Catriona Kelly
THE RUSSIAN REVOLUTION
    S. A. Smith
SCHIZOPHRENIA
    Chris Frith and Eve Johnstone
SCHOPENHAUER
    Christopher Janaway
SCIENCE AND RELIGION
    Thomas Dixon
SEXUALITY Véronique Mottier
SHAKESPEARE Germaine Greer
SIKHISM Eleanor Nesbitt

SOCIAL AND CULTURAL
    ANTHROPOLOGY
    John Monaghan and Peter Just
SOCIALISM Michael Newman
SOCIOLOGY Steve Bruce
SOCRATES C. C. W. Taylor
THE SPANISH CIVIL WAR
    Helen Graham
SPINOZA Roger Scruton
STUART BRITAIN John Morrill
TERRORISM Charles Townshend
THEOLOGY David F. Ford
THE HISTORY OF TIME
    Leofranc Holford-Strevens
TRAGEDY Adrian Poole
THE TUDORS John Guy
TWENTIETH-CENTURY
    BRITAIN Kenneth O. Morgan
THE UNITED NATIONS
    Jussi M. Hanhimäki
THE VIETNAM WAR
    Mark Atwood Lawrence
THE VIKINGS Julian Richards
WITTGENSTEIN A. C. Grayling
WORLD MUSIC Philip Bohlman
THE WORLD TRADE
    ORGANIZATION
    Amrita Narlikar

Available soon:

APOCRYPHAL GOSPELS
    Paul Foster
CATHOLICISM Gerald O'Collins
EXPRESSIONISM
    Katerina Reed-Tsocha
FREE SPEECH Nigel Warburton
LINCOLN Allen C. Guelzo
MODERN JAPAN
    Christopher Goto-Jones

NOTHING Frank Close
PHILOSOPHY OF RELIGION
    Jack Copeland
    and Diane Proudfoot
RELATIVITY Russell Stannard
SCOTLAND Rab Houston
STATISTICS David Hand
SUPERCONDUCTIVITY
    Stephen Blundell

For more information visit our websites
www.oup.com/uk/vsi
www.oup.com/us

Kyle Keefer

# THE NEW TESTAMENT AS LITERATURE

## A Very Short Introduction

Wilbraham Public Library
25 Crane Park Drive
Wilbraham, MA 01095

OXFORD
UNIVERSITY PRESS

# OXFORD
UNIVERSITY PRESS

Oxford University Press, Inc., publishes works that further
Oxford University's objective of excellence
in research, scholarship, and education.

Oxford  New York
Auckland  Cape Town  Dar es Salaam  Hong Kong  Karachi
Kuala Lumpur  Madrid  Melbourne  Mexico City  Nairobi
New Delhi  Shanghai  Taipei  Toronto

With offices in
Argentina  Austria  Brazil  Chile  Czech Republic  France  Greece
Guatemala  Hungary  Italy  Japan  Poland  Portugal  Singapore
South Korea  Switzerland  Thailand  Turkey  Ukraine  Vietnam

Copyright © 2008 by Kyle Keefer

Published by Oxford University Press, Inc.
198 Madison Avenue, New York, NY 10016

www.oup.com

Oxford is a registered trademark of Oxford University Press

All rights reserved. No part of this publication may be reproduced,
stored in a retrieval system, or transmitted, in any form or by any means,
electronic, mechanical, photocopying, recording, or otherwise,
without the prior permission of Oxford University Press.

Library of Congress Cataloging-in-Publication Data
Keefer, Kyle.
The New Testament as literature : a very short introduction / Kyle Keefer.
p.  cm.
Includes bibliographical references and index.
ISBN 978-0-19-530020-8 (pbk.)
1. Bible. N.T.—Criticism, interpretation, etc.
2. Bible as literature. I. Title.
BS2361.3.K44 2008
225.6'1—dc22
2008014435

3 4 5 6 7 8 9
Printed in Great Britain on acid-free paper
by Ashford Colour Press Ltd, Gosport, Hampshire

# Contents

# Acknowledgments

Thanks to Cybele Tom at Oxford University Press for guiding this project through with patience and care. To Tod Linafelt, Tim Beal, Chris Boesel, Brent Plate, Mary Foskett, Wes Allen, and the rest of my former Emory colleagues, thanks for the conversations. I'll always be grateful for how they inform all my work, including this one.

# Chapter 1
# Introduction

Any reader of the New Testament traverses well-worn ground. The twenty-seven individual writings that date from 2000 years ago carry with them centuries of interpretation. Millions of Westerners—and as Christianity continues to spread in Africa and Asia, vast numbers of people in the Eastern and Southern Hemispheres—have felt the influence of the content of the New Testament. The Christian Bible, comprised of the New Testament and the Hebrew Bible (also known as the Old Testament), has been read by more groups and individuals than any other book ever written.

This panoply of readers, current and past, approaches the New Testament from a variety of perspectives. Most commonly, Christian readers read the New Testament religiously; they assume that their reading will provide guidance for their beliefs and actions. But Christian devotional readers are by no means the only type of readers. Followers of other religions—Jews or Buddhists, for example—read for cross-cultural religious understanding. The questions they bring to their reading may be similar to those of Christians, but from an outsider's perspective. Nonreligious or antireligious people also read the New Testament, often with an aim to point out fallacies or shortcomings of the text. Inevitably, the types of questions a reader brings to the New Testament will affect the interpretation.

I am looking at the New Testament through a very particular lens, that of literary study. The questions raised here focus on the language and craft of the text itself. A literary approach to the New Testament assumes that the documents found here not only convey ideas but also entertain, prod, puzzle, and delight audiences. Even for readers not religiously bound to the New Testament, the artistry of the New Testament can prove engaging and provocative. Reading the New Testament as literature brings to light the dynamics of this engagement. Whereas religious interpreters of these scriptures, driven by a desire to find moral or theological content, might overlook the aesthetic experience of the reader, literary interpretation foregrounds this experience.

The literary approach dominates in many courses that go by the title "The Bible as Literature." The word "as" in that description, however, is ambiguous. It could condition readers to approach the Bible as they would other literary works. That is, a reader will attune himself or herself to plot, syntax, character development, and rhetoric. Therefore, one sense of "the Bible as literature" refers to the *content* of the text. Such standard literary features are main concerns of this book, and I elaborate on them in this first chapter. But the "as" could also imply a reevaluation of the Bible, one that would insert it into the literary canon. In this second sense, the "as" relates to the *function* of the text. In the second chapter I address the relationship between the New Testament and the literature.

The early readers of the New Testament, perhaps surprisingly, were eager to distinguish it *from* literature. Around the year 400, in his *Confessions*, Augustine recounts how his first encounter with Cicero, "whose writing nearly everyone admires," affected him so profoundly that he dedicated himself to philosophy. A few lines later, he contrasts this delight with his first reading of the Bible, which "seemed to me unworthy in comparison with the dignity of Cicero." Although Augustine praises the content of the Christian scriptures ("of mountainous difficulty and enveloped in mysteries"), he finds scriptural language rather ordinary ("a text lowly to the beginner"). He chastises himself, though, for his inability to grasp this paradox of the scriptures: "My inflated conceit shunned the Bible's restraint, and my gaze never penetrated to its inwardness."[1] Nevertheless, the prose of the New Testament itself does not enthrall Augustine.

Literary study of the New Testament must surely grapple with Augustine's dilemma. No writer of the New Testament thought he was composing literature in the sense of belles lettres. In fact, no reader even thought to apply the term "literature" to the New Testament until the nineteenth century. Augustine's "humble gait" label, however, underestimates the texts' verbal power. Because early Christian writers were eager to espouse the superiority of the New Testament over such works as the *Odyssey* or the *Aeneid* and because they hesitated to make their case stylistically, they drew a sharp separation between form and content, elevating the latter at the expense of the former. This emphasis on ideas left an indelible mark on Christianity, especially as literacy became an asset of a minority in the Middle Ages. With the landmark vernacular translations of the Bible (especially the King James Bible in 1611), the literary aspects of the text became increasingly important. Especially in the twentieth century, as scholars and readers began to attend more closely to the form of the writings, it became clear that the authorial skill of the New Testament writers had been greatly underestimated not only by Augustine but by the majority of Christian readers.

For most of Christian history, readers of the New Testament assumed that their reading would reveal God's truth to them. Devout Christians interacted personally with the text. They would not, as a modern read might, wonder about the medical facts surrounding Jesus' healing/exorcism of an epileptic (Mark 9:17–29, cf. Matt. 17:14–20, Luke 9:37–42) but instead would take the miracle at face value and then ponder how they too might experience healing or deliverance from demons. In the eighteenth and nineteenth centuries, however, biblical scholarship as an

3

academic enterprise approached the Bible objectively. The biblical scholars of the nineteenth century, primarily in Germany, attempted to free themselves from the strictures of dogmatic concerns. They thought of themselves as scientists who investigated the New Testament through the microscopes of history. Thus they read the text quite carefully and practiced a type of literary critique, but without much interest in either aesthetics or the dynamic interplay between text and reader. Scholars enacting this older type of literary criticism wanted to go behind the text to find out what the texts could tell them about the world from which they arose. They did, in fact, ask questions about the veracity of Jesus' healing and concluded that the story reflected not historical truth but the early church's claims about Jesus. They looked at how the form of the miracle stories in general resembled folklore, and thus the stories said more about the people who transmitted them than about Jesus himself.

For a multitude of reasons, this historical method no longer dominates academic investigation of the New Testament. As scholars (and, more importantly, their students) realized that the historical approach often alienates readers from the Bible, literary approaches to the New Testament came to the fore in academic discourse. What was so refreshing about the rise of literary approaches was that it could (and can) appeal to nonspecialists. Most readers, now and in the past, simply do not read to develop historical acuity. Biblical scholars, because of the way they formulated their work, had created a gulf between themselves and the vast majority of New Testament readers. Literary readings of the New Testament help bridge this gulf by avoiding the extremes of objectivity and subjectivity. A literary reading will, for example, explore the pathos of the epileptic boy and the characterization of Jesus. Through aesthetic appreciation, someone can personally engage the New Testament without necessarily feeling the need to learn a moral lesson. Even if the New Testament authors did not envision themselves as rivals of Virgil, they ended up creating literature nonetheless. Like great literature, the New Testament writings have become part of the story-world of those who read them. A literary approach, therefore, seems commensurate with the actual experience of modern readers.

An example can illuminate the aesthetic appeal of the New Testament and the advantages of literary analysis. One of the best-known stories in the New Testament is the parable of the Good Samaritan. When speakers of English use the phrase "Good Samaritan," they denote a kindhearted person who helps another person in distress. Even if such speakers have never read Luke 10:25–37, they intuit that the story gives an example of action to be followed. As much as any story in the New Testament, this parable has proved to resonate with audiences. A literary reading of the story, while not contradicting the received wisdom about this parable, highlights the layers of the story that contribute to its appeal.

The parable is structured around different rounds of questions and answers between Jesus and an inquisitive lawyer:

[Lawyer] "Teacher, what must I do to inherit eternal life?"
[Jesus] "What is written in the law? What do you read there?"
[Lawyer] "You shall love the Lord your God with all your heart, and
  with all your soul, and with all your strength, and with all your
  mind, and your neighbor as yourself."
[Jesus] "You have given the right answer; do this, and you will live."
[Lawyer] "And who is my neighbor?"
[Jesus] "A man was going down from Jerusalem to Jericho, and fell
  into the hands of robbers, who stripped him, beat him, and went
  away, leaving him half dead. Now by chance a priest was going
  down that road; and when he saw him he passed by on the other
  side. So likewise a Levite, when he came to the place and saw him,
  passed by on the other side. But a Samaritan while traveling came
  upon him; and when he saw him, he was moved with pity. He went
  to him and bandaged his wounds, having poured oil and wine on
  them. Then he put him on his own animal and brought him to an
  inn, and took care of him. The next day he took out two denarii,

gave them to the innkeeper, and said, 'Take care of him, and when I come back, I will repay you whatever more you spend.' Which of these three, do you think, was a neighbor to the man who fell into the hands of the robbers?"

[Lawyer]: "The one who showed him mercy."

This exchange begins with agreement between the lawyer and Jesus about the necessity to love one's neighbor. But the lawyer immediately questions the semantic range of "neighbor," and a possible disagreement arises about who ought to be the recipient of the love. The parable Jesus tells in response centers on the definition of "neighbor," and Jesus cleverly redirects the original question. The lawyer, now having to answer his own query, equates "neighbor" with "one who showed him mercy." The conclusion of the parable gives an unexpected twist to the story, but only if the logic of the dialogue is followed carefully:

[Lawyer] "I know I should love my neighbor, but who is my neighbor?"

[Jesus] "Here's a story about a beaten man and a Samaritan. Now you tell me who the neighbor is."

[Lawyer] "The Samaritan."

[Jesus] "Then you should love that Samaritan, the outcast who comes to your aid."

If one should love a neighbor, and if the Samaritan plays the role of "neighbor," then the lawyer should love the Samaritan. Furthermore, if the lawyer must love the Samaritan, the lawyer identifies *not* with the giver of mercy but with the recipient of it. In other words, he must follow the example not of the Samaritan but, surprisingly, of the beaten man, who takes no action at all. He must be willing to love the despised neighbor (Samaritans were the object of strong racism at the time of Jesus) who becomes his benefactor.

Notice that this literary reading of the story runs contrary to popular interpretation in which the Good Samaritan stands as the example to follow. That reading becomes possible with a line I have so far omitted, when Jesus says, "Go and do likewise." Here Jesus does enjoin the lawyer to take action. But what type? "Likewise" might refer to the Samaritan's action, but Jesus does not make such an identification clear. The ambiguous ending hints that the lawyer is asked to take on two roles at once, both to show mercy and to receive mercy lovingly. To read the parable simply as a story about a do-gooder misses this complexity.

Too often the New Testament's writings are similarly assumed to have simplistic meanings. Literary readings awaken us to the intricacies of the language that makes up the New Testament. We should guard against taking Augustine's (and scholarship's) viewpoint to the extreme, emphasizing content as the kernel to savor while discarding the husk of the words themselves. A literary reading of the New Testament allows readers to understand content through close engagement with form.

In chapters 3 through 5, I explore the major sections of the New Testament—the gospels, Paul's letters, and Revelation—as literary documents. Then, I step back and ask questions about the New Testament as a whole. Whether read as a singular document or as a collection of parts, the New Testament presents readers with a variety of forms and viewpoints, and a literary exploration helps bring this multivalence to light.

A final note about the issue of translation. Since we live in an era in which we can read works in a plethora of languages through translation, this problem may not seem acute. Still, translation always distorts the original text at least somewhat, and one cannot perform as close a reading of the New Testament in English as one could in Greek, the original language of the New Testament. When necessary and useful, I will refer to the original language, but in a more general sense, word patterns and narrative structure are very accessible in the modern English translations that I use. Unless otherwise marked, I quote from the New Revised Standard Version (NRSV). Sometimes I will use the King James Version (KJV) or my own translation, which I note clearly.

The New Testament as Literature

# Chapter 2
# The New Testament and the literary canon

## What counts as literature?

The title of this book raises the pertinent question: "What does it mean to read literature?" or more specifically, "What is literature?" In the first chapter, I pointed out how one might appropriate the New Testament as literature, but can we simply call any work literature? Many people, upon hearing the word, think of it as some type of prose or poetry that surpasses other writing in its quality. They might remember works they were assigned to read in college or high school (and very possibly do not read anymore . . . ). Reading literature, as opposed to other types of writing, implies a serious undertaking, unlike reading comics or the newspaper.

Thinking of literature this way—as a consciously aesthetic, high-minded activity—does not necessarily work when applied to the New Testament. As we've already seen, readers of the New Testament have judged it to be much *less* self-consciously polished than works in the literary canon. The Gospel of Matthew, for example, does not favorably compare with *Moby Dick* with regard to linguistic complexities we often associate with literary works. The definition of literature as art for art's sake, however, is fairly recent and too limiting. If there seems to be cognitive dissonance involved in thinking of the New Testament as literature, the problem lies not so much with the biblical text as with the preconceived notion of what counts as literature.

But if literature is not defined by the intrinsic quality of "literariness," whatever that is, how should it be defined? I propose that we think of literature according to its effects on its readers, or, more simply, according to its function. Here I refer to Kenneth Burke, a twentieth-century literary critic. He wrote an essay whose title is his thesis, "Literature as Equipment for Living." Burke takes a pragmatic approach to literature, as opposed to an aesthetic one, and demonstrates how individuals *use* literature in their everyday life. His examples range from proverbs to poems to Aesop's fables to dictionary entries. Through all these examples, he emphasizes how literature helps humans adapt to and respond to situations they face. He proposes that we think of literary works as

> strategies for selecting enemies and allies, for socializing losses, for warding off evil eye, for purification, propitiation, and desanctification, consolation and vengeance, admonition and exhortation, implicit commands or instructions of one sort or another. Art forms like "tragedy" or "comedy" or "satire" would be treated as *equipments for living*, that size up situations in various ways and in keeping with correspondingly various attitudes.[1]

In a different work, but in the same vein, Burke calls literature the "verbalization of experience." Great literature, therefore, equips humans for living, having verbalized in rich language those experiences that resonate with audiences throughout different eras. According to *this* understanding of literature, the New Testament certainly fits the bill.

## Using the New Testament

Burke implies that when a person reads a wide array of literature, he or she collects those literary experiences into a thesaurus or storehouse that can address particular situations. This sort of pragmatic reading of the New Testament happens all the time. Weary taxpayers moan that it is time to "render unto Caesar the things that are Caesar's," a quotation from Matthew. Upon seeing a criminal convicted, an observer might cluck her tongue and mutter, "You reap what you sow," a clear allusion to Galatians. In neither of the quotations does the interpreter of the text make a theological point, but in both the New Testament plays an important sociological role. As a text intricately tied to the West, the Bible is part of the cultural thesaurus, a source of cultural touchstones that millions of people share, irrespective of their religious beliefs.

Writers throughout Western history, until very recently, could assume that their readers would be able to understand their allusions to the Bible, even the most obscure ones. In 1681 John Dryden wrote a poem titled "Absalom and Achitophel," in which the poet addressed the crisis in England about who would succeed Charles II. The poem was printed in several editions and enjoyed a wide enough readership that it seems to have influenced the politics of his day. Dryden assumed then—he would probably not assume so today—that his audience would understand the referents in the poem. It retells, with slight variation, the story from the Hebrew Bible of King David, his son Absalom, and Achitophel, an adviser to the king's son. Dryden refers to almost every character in 2 Samuel, and his readers not only were able to follow this complex set of characters but also connect the biblical characters with English figures. The ancient Hebrew text served as the perfect tool for Dryden's satire because he shared with his readers a common knowledge of the referents. Without such an agreement between author and audience, Dryden's poem would have failed miserably as political satire.

Although biblical literacy is not as strong today as it has been historically, the New Testament, along with other classic literary works, contributes to the lingua franca, the common language of

Western civilization. To call a traitor a Judas differs little from calling an indecisive person Hamlet. In both situations, the speaker can assume that his or her hearer will have enough familiarity with the Bible or Shakespeare to make the names understandable. While the New Testament texts have often played a polemical role in doctrinal arguments, political battles, and religious instruction, they also have functioned as "equipment for living." When life situations demand reaction, the stories of the New Testament can be used to address and guide reactions. For instance, the book of Revelation has strongly influenced how Europeans and North Americans have coped with and interpreted imminent threats to their existence. From the bubonic plague to the Cold War, the apocalyptic overtones of Revelation have colored people's reactions to catastrophic events. Reading the New Testament as literature, moreover, opens up the text to an audience well outside the confines of a Christian audience. If the text serves as equipment for living, dogmatic belief about the sanctity of the text or its status as God's word is not a prerequisite for profitable engagement.

## The New Testament in literature

The sense of the Bible as a storehouse seems especially pertinent in the study of actual works of literature. Any list of great literary works in the West will be replete with books, plays, poems, and essays that draw from the Bible. Some of these—*Paradise Lost*, *Pilgrim's Progress*—have explicitly Christian themes while others—*Absalom, Absalom!*, *Ulysses*—allude to biblical language and themes undogmatically. Any reader attempting to appreciate Western literature without knowledge of the Bible will inevitably miss some of the depth in that literature, and recently in the United States schools have added the Bible to the curriculum in order to provide students useful cultural touchstones.

Recognizing biblical allusions, however, is only the first step; it is necessary to move beyond the bare fact of allusion to the analysis of how authors use the Bible. Exploring how authors have incorporated the Bible into their creations sheds light on the question of how contemporary readers might also appropriate the Bible in their own aesthetic appreciation of it. To read the New Testament as literature closely parallels the way that authors of literature use the text.

Consider the appropriation of the New Testament in Dante's *Divine Comedy*. As the pilgrim Dante descends into Hell and then ascends through Purgatory and Paradise, he meets a variety of individuals. The poet Dante drew from a wide-ranging stock, including historical figures from Rome (Cato, Virgil), his contemporary citizens of Florence (Brunetto Latini), mythological characters (Ulysses), Christian saints (Lucy, Francis), and biblical characters (Judas, Mary). The way that Dante incorporates all of these personae into his work indicates that he views them all as characters, drawing no distinctions between factual and imaginary ones. It strikes the modern reader as odd that he cares so little about differentiating between fact and legend, but in Dante's scheme, such a distinction becomes irrelevant. When it comes to using the New Testament to construct the tripartite otherworld of the *Commedia*, Dante treats the biblical text no differently than mythological texts or historical data. The New Testament does not stand on its own as an isolated work but rather, as in Burke's definition of literature, provides Dante with certain strategies for poetic creation. Another way to construe what it means to read the New Testament as literature is to say that a person like Dante thinks with the stories of the New Testament. They become part of the language used to make sense of the world.

A more detailed example of how an author kneads the New Testament into literature comes from Geoffrey Chaucer's *Canterbury Tales*. Of all the travelers to Canterbury, the Wife of Bath probably stands as the perennial favorite of later audiences. When her turn to regale the Canterbury pilgrims arrives, the Wife of Bath tells a fable centering on the ambiguous nature of power in romantic relations between men and women. Before this tale, however, she spins a prologue more than twice as long as her tale. In her prologue, the Wife, who Chaucer has already characterized as sensuous ("of remedies of love she knew per chaunce"), defends her five marriages and her uncanny knack for finding herself a widow. The joyous complexity of the Wife is reflected in both her prologue and her tale, but here I focus on the prologue because in it the Wife repeatedly appeals to the New Testament text. In his construction of the Wife, Chaucer presents a character in literature who reads the New Testament as a literary text in explicit defense of her manner of life—as equipment for living.

She begins her prologue, "Experience, though noon auctoritee / Were in this world, is right ynogh for me / To speke of wo that is in marriage." (If there were no authority on earth/Except experience—mine, for what it's worth, / And that's enough for me, all goes to show / That marriage is a misery and a woe)." This rebellion against authority would seemingly disavow any reliance upon biblical texts to support her position. It is therefore surprising that in the next seventy-five lines of her speech, she makes a dozen different references to the Bible to justify her experience. She highlights characters from the Hebrew Bible— Abraham, Jacob, and above all Solomon—who precede her in polygamy; if they could have multiple wives, she should be able to enjoy multiple husbands (hers, of course, are in succession, not simultaneous).

Her engagement with the New Testament, however, goes deeper than allusiveness and illustrations. She first refers to the Gospel of John, to an episode where Jesus attends a wedding. Others, the Wife says, have used this text to bolster the claim for one marriage only: "Sith that Crist ne wernte nevere but onis / To weddying, in the Cane of Galilee, / That by the same ensample taughte he me / That I ne sholde wedded by but ones." She counters this argument by pointing to a different passage in John in which Jesus meets a Samaritan woman who has been wed five times, the same number as the Wife. Why those who refer to Cana overlook this fact, the Wife cannot understand.

Later in the prologue, the Wife engages Paul on the topics of marriage, sexual activity, and celibacy. In the fourteenth century, Chaucer's time, the church's position on marriage was strongly influenced not only by the Bible but also by writers who argued that Christians—women especially—should strive for virginity and that within marriage, sexual activity should be performed only for the sake of producing children. The Wife of Bath, who wants to enjoy sex for its own sake as often as she pleases, contradicts the establishment view. She enrolls Paul for support, in order to demonstrate how poorly the church fathers have interpreted 1 Corinthians, where Paul writes:

> Now concerning the matters about which you wrote: "It is well for a man not to touch a woman." But because of cases of sexual immorality, each man should have his own wife, and each woman her own husband. The husband should give to his wife her conjugal rights, and likewise the wife to her husband. For the wife does not have authority over her own body, but the husband does; likewise, the husband does not have authority over his own body, but the wife does. Do not deprive one another except perhaps by agreement for a set time, to devote yourselves to prayer, and then come together again so that Satan may not tempt you because of your lack of self-control. This I say this by way of concession, not as a command. I wish that all were as I myself am. But each has a particular gift from God, one having one kind and another a different kind. To the unmarried and the widows I say that it is well for them to remain unmarried, as I am. But if they are not practicing self-control, they should marry. For it is better to marry than to be aflame with passion. (1 Cor. 7:1–9)

. . . . . . . . . . . .

> Now concerning virgins, I have no command from the Lord, but I give my opinion as one who by the Lord's mercy is trustworthy.

15

I think that, in view of the impending crisis, it is well for you to remain as you are. Are you bound to a wife? Do not seek to be free. Are you free from a wife? Do not seek a wife. But if you marry, you do not sin, and if a virgin marries, she does not sin. Yet those who marry will experience distress in this life, and I would spare you that. (1 Cor. 7:25–28)

In her prologue, the Wife refers to almost every single one of these verses. Essential to the Wife's self-assertion is the slipperiness of Paul's authority in 1 Corinthians. Because he does not have an absolutely clear command from God regarding virginity, he simply proposes advice. The Wife finds an opening here and pithily she says, "Conseillyng is no commandement." Paul's gift may have been virginity, but since he allows that all might not be as gifted as he, she will find her gift in marriage: "I wol bistowe the four of al myn age / In the actes and in fruyt of mariage." Moreover, going one step farther, Paul needs differently gifted women like the Wife in order for his counsel to flourish, for if all were virgins then virginity would die out. Or, as the Wife elegantly states the paradox, "For hadde God commanded maydenhede, / Thanne hadde he dampned weddyng with the dede / And certes, if ther were no seed ysowe, / Virginitee, thane wherof sholde it growe?" The Wife overlooks the irony of her childlessness here, but that does not negate the logic of her argument. Putting her words alongside Paul's opinions, one can observe great commonalities, and contrary to her opening statement, in which she divorces experience from authority, the Wife here valorizes her experience with reference to the authority of Paul.

The layers of interpretive complexity go even farther than what I have briefly outlined. How, for instance, in a culture that did not have printed English Bibles, does the Wife know these texts? Does she truly believe her own argument, or, like Chaucer's Pardoner, does she hoodwink her audience with self-aware hypocrisy? The points to make here are twofold. First, the Wife reads the New Testament as a strategic tool for her prologue. While she implicitly recognizes the canonical value of the text, she does not emphasize its sacredness and, somewhat jarringly for her context, brings the sacred into close contact with the secular. The Wife, in other words, reads the New Testament as literature, in the Burkean sense I previously described. Second, her interaction with Paul takes place on a textual plain, not a theological one. By this I mean that, to a great extent, the Wife engages 1 Corinthians through the type of close reading I was advocating in my first chapter. She is not so much rebelling against the church's position for rebellion's sake as she is demonstrating that she, by reading the text outside of a dogmatic context, can interpret the Bible better than the church fathers. Their problem—along with not truly understanding woman's experience—is that they are not actually reading the words of the New Testament itself.

## Conclusion

Literary appropriation of the New Testament like Chaucer's or Dante's helps defamiliarize the text away from a possibly limiting religious context. Neither Chaucer nor Dante is *antireligious,* but any religiosity in their works is couched in an artistic framework. In the hands of literary artists, the biblical text can appear more multifaceted and open to new possibilities than it does in explicitly religious readings. To read the New Testament as literature, therefore, is something of a creative act, probing the language and features of the text with an eye toward intentional dialogue, as opposed to a passive reception of theological truths.

# Chapter 3
# The gospels

## Gospels and biographies

If Jesus were to appear in our era, a biographer who wanted to capture his life in print would certainly compose something quite different from what we find in the New Testament. Modern audiences expect biographies to begin with the subject's childhood (sometimes the subject's parents' childhoods) and to continue through adolescence, young adulthood, and eventually death. (In the middle of the biography, readers might also find photographic plates to augment their textual interpretation.) Biographies rely heavily on factual details that can be clearly documented. If a biography (or autobiography) veers too far into an imaginative or literary portrait, it is likely to receive sharp criticism. Indeed, when reviewers critique biographies, it is usually because they find something factually wrong with the biographer's claims.

The New Testament opens with four narratives of Jesus that thwart the expectations of modern readers of biographies. These narratives, called gospels, do not worry much about chronology. Not a single physical aspect of Jesus is mentioned. (The closest one gets to photographic plates are imaginative art pieces, usually reserved for children's Bibles.) Except for some very brief episodes, we learn nothing about Jesus' childhood or adolescence.

The gospel writers do not attempt to psychologize Jesus either—they do not pretend to get inside his head to explain his motivations.

Although the gospels can therefore seem opaque, they are not thereby thin in content or style. All four present a remarkable figure, and each has its distinct manner of presentation. Many scholars assert that the gospels fit the genre of *ancient* biographies, a genre encompassing expectations much different from ours. Ancient biographers such as Plutarch and Suetonius present their subjects' lives not journalistically or factually but polemically. These ancient writers, when they sketch historical figures, do so with an aim to make a moral or didactic claim. Chronological accuracy, in this mode of writing, becomes subservient to the overarching thesis of the author. Anecdote in particular serves as an exemplary element of the Greek term *bios*. To use contemporary categories, we would view these Greek and Roman biographers as combining folklore, gossip, praise, and literary invention.

A reader who approaches the gospels looking for a factual, objective report of Jesus will inevitably be frustrated. The gospel writers resemble artists and/or polemicists more than journalists because they select material, style of presentation, structure, and terminology, all in the service of portraying a Jesus that they consider decisive. In the same way that we describe varieties of art works—music, painting, film—as compositions, the aesthetic implications of composing aptly describe the work of the gospel writers. They are compositors in the sense that they are gathering material that they have received, but they are also composing—placing and organizing—this material to suit their finished product. In other words, it does not make sense to separate ancient biography from literature. Neither Plutarch nor Suetonius, roughly contemporaries of the gospel writers, assumes that they are simply giving the reader a biographical subject "as they really were," whatever that phrase might mean.

# The historical aspects of the gospels

Although this chapter examines literary aspects of the gospels, it is necessary to synthesize briefly some tenets that New Testament scholars hold. In what follows, I assume four very basic conjectures about the gospels that are standard in New Testament scholarship:

A. That all four gospels were written sometime between 65 CE and 95 CE, at least thirty years after Jesus' crucifixion.

B. That all four were originally anonymous and that the names Matthew, Mark, Luke, and John were added later. These author names serve as convenient fictions (i.e., I call the author of the first gospel "Matthew," but this name does not designate the apostle known by that name).

C. That none of the gospel writers witnessed the events recounted in the gospels.

D. That each writer was dependent on sources, both written and oral.

There are certainly other standard assumptions of New Testament critics, relating to audience, historicity, and compositional history, but such assumptions often obfuscate rather than enhance a literary appreciation of the texts. As much as possible, I am confining myself to aesthetics. A reader of the New Testament very likely will have questions about the historical accuracy of the gospels, but addressing those concerns would be misplaced in this analysis.

## The Synoptic Gospels

If one reads Matthew, Mark, and Luke next to one another, they look remarkably similar. Here is a short passage found in all three gospels:

| Matthew 19:13–15 | Mark 10:13–16 | Luke 18:15–17 |
| --- | --- | --- |

Then children were brought to him in order that he might lay hands upon them and pray for them. But the disciples rebuked them. But Jesus said, "Allow the children to come to me and do not hinder them, for the kingdom of heaven belongs to such as these." And after he laid hands upon them, he departed that place. (author's translation)

And they brought children to him in order that he might touch them. But the disciples rebuked them. But Jesus, seeing this, was indignant and said to them, "Allow the children to come to me; do not hinder them, for the kingdom of God belongs to such as these. Truly I tell you, whoever does not receive the kingdom of God as a child will never enter it." And he blessed them, putting his arms around them and laying his hands on them. (author's translation)

And they brought babies to him in order that he might touch them. But seeing this, the disciples rebuked them. But Jesus invited them, saying, "Allow the children to come to me, and do not hinder them, for the kingdom of God belongs to such as these. Truly I tell you, whoever does not receive the kingdom of God as a child will never enter it." (author's translation)

There are hundreds of examples like these, passages or sentences that appear in all three of these gospels with slight variations. In this example, Mark and Matthew use the word "children," while Luke describes them as "babies." Matthew is missing the last statement found in Mark and Luke, and he says "kingdom of heaven" instead of "kingdom of God."

How do we explain these commonalities? Suppose that a teacher had given a class a writing assignment and Matthew, Mark, and Luke all handed in their work with verbal similarities like the ones above. The teacher would immediately suspect that somebody had copied (though she or he would not know who copied whom). This supposition, which seems the most obvious explanation, is the most widely held account of the similarities among Matthew, Mark, and Luke. Mark, the shortest gospel, was written first, and then later Matthew and Luke used Mark as an outline when they wrote their own gospels. Because of such similarities, we call these three gospels the Synoptics, which means "to see together." (John does not copy from the Synoptics and his gospel differs dramatically from the first three.)

The intricacies of exactly how Mark, Matthew, and Luke relate to one another can be a lifelong pursuit. For a literary reading, however, the interrelationship of the Synoptics has only one primary interest, and it relates to Matthew and Luke. If Matthew and Luke use Mark as a guide, when they differ from Mark, they have made an interpretive choice. While it is not necessary to refer to Synoptic overlap in a literary reading of Matthew and Luke—and many literary studies of the gospels do not—it can be illuminating. The distinctive art of a writer that uses sources, however, becomes more manifest if the reader knows how the writer altered those sources. Many facets of Shakespeare's plays, for instance, come into sharper relief when one compares his dramas with Holinshed's *Chronicles*, a historical source he used extensively for plays such as *Macbeth* and *Henry IV*. Knowing that Matthew and Luke reworked Mark can enrich our literary investigation of both of the later gospels.

# Mark

The Gospel of Mark, the shortest of the four, presents an enigmatic portrait of Jesus in a very terse narrative. It opens with the briefest of introductions ("The beginning of the gospel of Jesus Christ, Son of God" [1:1]) and closes with an ambiguous conclusion ("They said nothing to anyone, for they were afraid [16:8]). In between, the narrative moves at a rapid pace, presenting a montage of Jesus' actions and words, all arranged as a series of short episodes, except for the climax, when he tells the story of Jesus' death and crucifixion.

The style and structure of Mark have led readers to label it with a variety of adjectives—terse, enigmatic, clumsy, prolix, subtle, simplistic, unadorned. It can be argued (and has been argued by many) that the sparseness of the gospel is due simply to the author's decision to act as a chronicler who shows little concern with literary craft. Contrarily, one can read Mark as a Hemingwayesque novelist, who utilizes straightforward narrative and dialogue to present a complex but subtle portrait of Jesus. Neither of these descriptions precisely captures Mark's gospel, but both have some truth to them. Regardless of authorial intent, as it stands, the Gospel of Mark consistently presents a Jesus that resists facile comprehension or simplistic interpretation.

The first impressions of Jesus portray a figure strikingly different from any other first-century Galilean. Mark simply calls him "Son of God" in the first verse, but he does not explain the status of this sonship. Mark eschews discussion of Jesus' birth or boyhood and by means of this epigram succinctly presents Jesus as a divine figure. In a modern biography, the biographer would trace patterns of interaction between the subject and his environment in order to highlight the subject's distinctive features. Mark simply proclaims Jesus' uniqueness. After Jesus exorcises a demon in the middle of the synagogue, onlookers express their astonishment: "What is this? A new teaching—with authority! He commands even the unclean spirits, and they obey him" (1:27). Both the narrator and the crowd agree that no one else resembles Jesus.

But as the gospel progresses, it becomes increasingly difficult to know what sort of person Jesus wants to present to the world. He performs miracles and then warns people not to tell anyone about his supernatural abilities. Through such acts and through preaching, he draws crowds to himself, but he then withdraws from the people attracted to him. He even separates himself from his own family. They first appear in chapter 3, when they try to "restrain him, for people were saying, 'He has gone out of his mind.' " Instead of mollifying their anxiety, he publicly disowns them. When told that his family is looking for him, Jesus rhetorically asks, "Who are my mother and my brothers?" He then answers his own question, "Whoever does the will of God is my brother and sister and mother" (3:21–35). To call Jesus lonely would be an overstatement—very rarely does Mark comment on Jesus' thoughts—but he is certainly alone. By the end of the gospel, everyone he knows has deserted him, even God. As he cries out, "My God, my God, why have you forsaken me?" (15:34), none of his acquaintances provide any moral support. There are only a few women, "looking on from a distance" (15:40).

Mark's gospel pays particular attention to the alienation that Jesus feels from his disciples. A key passage for investigating the dynamics of Mark occurs in chapter four, when Jesus articulates his first parable. He speaks of a sower who scatters seed on four different types of terrain. Mostly the seed falls on ground that proves inhospitable for germination and only a fourth of the seed actually sprouts. Jesus concludes the parable with the exhortation, "Let anyone with ears to hear listen!" Although Mark does not narrate the response of the crowd, he does tell the disciples' reaction, and they pointedly lack "ears to hear." Jesus responds to their request for an explanation: "To you has been given the mystery of the kingdom of God, but for those outside, everything comes in parables, in order that 'while seeing, they see but do not perceive, and while hearing, they hear but do not understand; so that they may not turn again and be forgiven'" (4:11–12). Instead of explaining himself, Jesus gives a justification for his parables, and this justification divides insiders from outsiders. In the hyperbole of this explanation, *everything* sounds parabolic to outsiders *in order that* they will remain outside. Jesus in Mark's gospel, according to his own admission, intentionally confounds his listeners to push them away.

The disciples would seem to play the role of insiders, in contrast to the scribes and other opponents, but this is not exactly right. Their privileged position only allows them the "mystery," not necessarily understanding. Some translations of this sentence read "secret" instead of mystery, but the Greek word is *mysterion* and the English derivative *mystery* better conveys Jesus' intent. This gift of mystery proves a mixed blessing for the disciples. Jesus asks in 4:13 a pair of questions: "Do you not understand this parable?" and "How then will you understand all the parables?" The answer to the first is "no" and to the second, the implied response is that they won't. The insiders have no more luck than the outsiders in comprehending Jesus' riddling speech. After Jesus speaks more parables about seeds, Mark states, "With many such parables he spoke the word to them, as they were able to hear it; he did not speak to them except in parables, but explained everything in private to his disciples" (4:33). The parable of the sower epitomizes Jesus' teaching to his disciples. He presents a parable that confounds them, and when they ask for explanation, they become only more confused. Returning to Jesus' questions, we can see that if the disciples do not understand the one parable, then they necessarily cannot understand all the parables.

The disciples never understand all the parables, and one can make the case that they never understand *any* of the parables. The characterization of the disciples in Mark's gospel is shocking in its condescension; the disciples are complete, utter dullards. One scene in particular makes this point. Mark narrates two stories of Jesus' miraculously feeding a crowd of thousands. The first, in Mark 6: 30–44, includes 5,000 men (plus presumably, commensurate numbers of women and children), and they all get their fill from five loaves of bread and two fish. After the meal, the disciples gather up twelve baskets of leftovers. In 8:1–10, presumably a short time later, Jesus does it again. This time he feeds 4,000 people with seven loaves and "a few" small fish (whatever "few" means, there must be more than two). This seemingly repetitive story serves primarily to point to the disciples' woeful comprehension. Three times in the first story, the place where the crowd gathers is described as deserted. In the second story, Jesus subtly urges the disciples to remember the previous feeding: "I have compassion for the crowd, because they have been with me now for three days and have nothing to eat. If I send them away hungry to their homes, they will faint on the way" (8:2–3). This statement cries out for the disciples to say, "Why don't you feed them the way that you did that other crowd." But instead they say "How can one feed these people with bread here in the desert?" (8:4). The syntax of their question amply demonstrates their cloddishness. A reader of the text wants to say in response, "The same way that one fed those people back in chapter six with the other *bread* in the other *deserted* place!"

But Mark does not let the disciples off the hook yet. He reserves one more jab. After this feeding, Jesus has a brief dispute with the Pharisees, in which he discusses "signs." What follows is a comical scene resembling a schoolteacher at wit's end with his students:

> Now the disciples had forgotten to bring any bread; and they had only one loaf with them in the boat. And he cautioned them, saying, "Watch out—beware of the yeast of the Pharisees and the yeast of Herod." They said to one another, "It is because we have no bread." And becoming aware of it, Jesus said to them, "Why are you talking

about having no bread? Do you still not perceive or understand? Are
your hearts hardened? Do you have eyes, and fail to see? Do you
have ears, and fail to hear? And do you not remember? When I
broke the five loaves for the five thousand, how many baskets full of
broken pieces did you collect?" They said to him, "Twelve." "And the
seven for the four thousand, how many baskets full of broken pieces
did you collect?" And they said to him, "Seven." Then he said to
them, "Do you not yet understand?" (8:14–21)

Jesus' series of questions recalls almost precisely the language of
4:12, and the disciples act exactly as outsiders because while seeing,
they do not see, and while hearing, they do not hear. The answer to
the last question, just as it had been in chapter 4, is emphatically
"No." Heavy irony pervades this passage, to the detriment of the
disciples. After Jesus has just been speaking about "signs," they
mistake a metaphorical statement for a literal truth. After just
having seen Jesus feed 4,000 people with seven loaves, they worry
that one loaf will not be enough for the twelve of them. The
mathematical lesson at the end shows that they can get their facts
right, but their interpretive skills are nil.

Jesus' almost constant frustration with the disciples and their
amazing ability to misunderstand pulls the reader in two
directions. In one sense, Mark encourages admiration and even
worship of Jesus. Rarely do narratives spotlight one particular
character—as Mark's gospel does—without portraying the
antagonist sympathetically. Because Jesus has many attractive
qualities, readers do tend to take his side and thus share in his
frustration over the disciples' stupidity. Yet the reader might also
side with the disciples. This would especially be true within a
religious community that already adhered to Christianity. In this
second sense of sympathetic reading, the reader would share in the
puzzlement that the disciples feel. Readers who do not claim any
religious connection with Mark can be as easily confounded by
Jesus as the disciples in the narrative are. By pushing the reader
both toward the uncomprehending disciples and the enigmatic

Jesus, the Gospel of Mark tends to destabilize the reader and to make the narrative just as challenging as its protagonist.

To put it another way, the Gospel of Mark creates paradox, and nowhere is the paradoxical nature of the gospel more apparent than in the events that lead up to Jesus' death. Almost immediately after this discourse with the disciples, Jesus begins to focus upon his impending death. Again gathering the disciples together for a private session, Jesus tells them that "the Son of Man must endure great suffering and be rejected by the elders and chief priests and scribes, be put to death and rise up three days later" (8:31). Twice more, with slight variations (9:31 and 10:33), he predicts his doom. This triad, often called Mark's "triple passion prediction," is one of the most obvious literary markers of the gospel. Mark's triple statement highlights the most important characterization of Jesus in this gospel: he is the suffering Son of Man.

Mark also uses these predictions to further characterize the disciples. After the first one, Mark adds the editorial comment, "And he spoke to them plainly." Yet they continue to misapprehend him. Their three reactions to Jesus' distressed predictions are: to rebuke him (8:32), to argue among themselves about who was greatest (9:34), and to ask for privileges once Jesus achieves his glory (10:37–40). The rebuke of Jesus by Simon Peter in 8:32 expresses confusion, but the other two border on callousness. In the face of the imminent death of their teacher, all they concern themselves with are their own rewards and security.

It must be said, however, that although Jesus explains very clearly *that* he is going to die, he never spells out *why* his sufferings must occur. While other books in the New Testament fill in this gap, in Mark the purpose of Jesus' suffering and death remain opaque. It is not surprising, therefore, that the disciples—perhaps not the brightest students to begin with—recoil at Jesus' strange insistence on his death. The crucifixion itself becomes one more parable that they do not understand. In fact, only one character in the entirety of the gospel does understand, and he shares only a few moments with Jesus. At the cross, the centurion who presides over the execution "saw that in this way he breathed his last" and proclaims, "Truly this man was God's son." This proclamation, made on the basis of whatever is meant by "in this way," recalls the very first words of the gospel, when Mark called Jesus "Son of God." This centurion is the only human character to agree publicly with Mark's initial designation.

Mark's literary style and his characterization of Jesus reinforce one another. The sparseness of the narrative contributes to the enigma of Jesus himself. In the same way that the narrative isolates the character of Jesus, thus also the syntax of the gospel isolates the reader. The end of the gospel makes this clear. In some manuscripts the gospel includes postresurrection appearances of Jesus in which he gives the disciples a farewell speech. In the earliest manuscripts, however, Mark's gospel ends at 16:8. While it is possible that the gospel was truncated—it would have been odd to conclude with the conjunction "for" as the gospel does— most versions of the text take this as the ending. If this were a play, it would end with an empty stage; as a text, the reader is left alone. Just as Jesus has been isolated throughout the gospel, yet continually puzzling his audience, the gospel itself concludes by compounding the mystery, almost as if it were challenging the reader with the same sorts of questions that Jesus poses to the disciples.

## Matthew

Toward the end of Matthew's gospel, Jesus gathers his disciples to celebrate the Passover meal. During the meal, he announces that one of them will betray him. Then the disciples "became greatly distressed and began to say to him one after another, 'Surely not I, Lord?' " Jesus replied that the one who "dipped his hand into the bowl" with him would be the betrayer. Apparently, the one sharing the bowl was Judas because he responds, "Surely not I, Rabbi?" In an abrupt ending to this scene, Jesus obliquely replies to Judas's question, "You have said so." (26:17–25)

What did Judas say? Without any contextual clues, Jesus' response seems opaque. Throughout his gospel, however, Matthew has carefully chosen the appellations that various characters use when addressing Jesus. Those who willingly follow Jesus almost always address him with the Greek title "kurios," which means either Lord or master (e.g., 8:2–8, 9:27–31, 14:28, 17:4, 20:30). Conversely, the characters antagonistic to Jesus often call him "teacher," a designation never used by Jesus' followers (e.g., 8:19, 12:38, 17:24, 19:16, 22:16). The contrasting responses of the disciples ("Surely not I, Lord?") and Judas ("Surely not I, Rabbi?") epitomize the contrast between devoted followers and interested outsiders that Matthew has built up in the course of his narrative. Matthew has carefully provided a narrative clue for his readers—all they need to know about a character's loyalty to Jesus is contained in how that character addresses him. To a discerning ear, Judas obviously indicts himself with his noun choice by calling Jesus "Rabbi" (the Hebrew word for "my teacher") during the meal. Shortly afterward, in Gethsemane, Judas commits a double act of betrayal with his proverbial kiss and with his words, both of which are acts of rich irony. The gospel pithily tells the story:

> Now the betrayer had given them a sign, saying, "The one I will kiss is the man; arrest him." At once he came up to Jesus and said, "Greetings, Rabbi!" and kissed him. Jesus said to him, "Friend, do what you are here to do." Then they came and laid hands on Jesus and arrested him. (26:48–50)

There is no need to suppose that Jesus had a supernatural ability to read Judas's intentions; his words serve as code language that fully signifies his treachery. To the armed crowd, Judas gives an agreed-upon sign (the kiss), but to Jesus and the attentive reader, he gives no less a sign—the word "Rabbi." Judas is the only character in Matthew to use either one.

This characterization of Judas points to one of the clearest stylistic features of Matthew's rhetoric—his penchant for sharp dualisms. Matthew's narrative often divides the world into two groups, and these divisions accomplish what Judas's question does, separating out Jesus' followers from his opponents. This care to draw shibboleths, dividing insiders from outsiders, pervades the gospel of Matthew. A few examples of Matthean divisions, in narrative order are: the narrow and the wide gates (chap. 7), the house on the rock and the house on sand (chap. 7), the parable of the wheat and the weeds (chap. 13), the parable of foolish and wise bridesmaids (chap. 25), and the allegory of the sheep and the goats (chap. 25). In each of these cases Matthew divides humanity into neat pairs, those who listen to Jesus' words, and those who do not. Unlike Mark's gospel, which tends to create imbalance in the reader because the line between insider and outsider is blurred, Matthew's gospel exudes clarity.

The best example of Matthean dualism appears at the conclusion of ethical teaching commonly called the "Sermon on the Mount" (chaps. 5–7), when Jesus supplies an exhortation that functions as a thesis statement to Matthew's gospel:

> Everyone then who hears these words of mine and acts on them will be like a wise man who built his house on rock. The rain fell, the floods came, and the winds blew and beat on that house, but it did not fall, because it had been founded on rock. And everyone who hears these words of mine and does not act on them will be like a foolish man who built his house on sand. The rain fell, and the floods came, and the winds blew and beat against that house, and it fell—and great was its fall! (7:24–27)

As the rest of Matthew makes clear, these two houses are the only available real estate options. It's an all-or-nothing proposition. The dichotomies Matthew presents generally include both an obvious reward and a disastrous punishment. With the two houses, it belabors the obvious to argue that a house built on sand is less

31

desirable than one with a foundation. It is clear which of these two would attract a potential dweller. But Matthew's Jesus, to hammer home his point, intensifies the difference by recounting the demolishment of the sand-based house. Throughout the gospel, punishment and reward reinforce one another, and Matthew rarely includes one without the other. The narrow gate promises life while the wide gate leads to destruction. In the parable of the wheat and the weeds, not only is the wheat harvested but the weeds are burned up. While wise bridesmaids are rewarded in their parable, the foolish ones are shut out of the wedding celebration. In a final judgment allegory, followers of Jesus (the sheep) enter into God's kingdom while those who do not listen to Jesus (the goats) enter into "the fire prepared for the devil and his angels."

Six times in the gospel, Matthew employs the stock phrase "weeping and gnashing of teeth" (8:12, 13:42, 13:50, 22:13, 24:51, 25:30) to indicate suffering under punishment. Two of these phrases occur in parables already mentioned (wheat and weeds, sheep and goats). The strangest appearance of the phrase comes at the end of a story that does not especially lend itself to punishment. In chapter 22, Jesus tells a parable about a king who hosted a wedding feast for his son. On the day of the feast, the invited guests back out, and some go so far as to murder the king's servants. In retaliation, the king kills the ungracious guests and invites others to take their place. The parable reaches its conclusion when the king's servants "went out into the streets and gathered together all whom they found, both good and bad; so the wedding hall was filled with dinner guests" (22:10). In other versions of this parable (in Luke and the apocryphal Gospel of Thomas), the gathering of this new set of guests ends the story. Matthew, though, cannot abide a mix of "good and bad," so in his gospel we find this coda:

> But when the king came in to see the guests, he noticed a man there who was not wearing a wedding robe, and he said to him, "Friend, how did you get in here without a wedding robe?" And he was

speechless. Then the king said to the attendants, "Bind him hand and foot, and throw him into the outer darkness, where there will be weeping and gnashing of teeth." For many are called, but few are chosen. (22:11–14)

This ending raises some intriguing questions. If many are called but few chosen, why call them to a banquet where they are going to be bounced out? Where was this person supposed to get a garment, and did he know such attire was required? (Probably not, since the king's servants simply "gathered all whom they found.") These questions cannot be answered presently, but simply raising them indicates the general framework of Matthew's storytelling. Even if the narrative logic does not call for a clear delineation of insider from outsider, Matthew crafts his episodes so that his dualistic framework remains intact.

Stylistically, therefore, Matthew has composed a gospel that creates a taxonomy of good and evil. In Jesus' words, "Whoever is not with me is against me, and whoever does not gather with me scatters" (12:30). Because of this structure, the tone of his gospel is surprisingly different from Mark's, even though the two share much of the same content. While Mark's authorial voice is muted and enigmatic, Matthew writes with earnestness and absolute surety.

Some changes that Matthew makes to Mark's gospel illustrate his desire for certainty. When Jesus explains to the disciples why he speaks in parables in Mark 4:11, he says, "To you has been given the mystery of the kingdom of God." This statement carries too much ambiguity for Matthew, who changes it to "To you it has been given *to know* the mysteries of the Kingdom of Heaven" (13:11, emphasis added). After the parable of the sower in Mark, Jesus says, "Do you not understand this parable?" with an understood answer of "No" on the disciples' part. In Matthew's gospel, after attaching many more parables to the parable of the sower, Jesus asks the disciples, "Have you understood all this?"

to which they reply confidently, "Yes" (13:51). For Matthew, solid knowledge is a necessity, and he gives clear instructions on how to achieve it. Whereas Mark's portrayal of the disciples puts into question the easy categorization of insiders and outsiders, Matthew's leaves no doubt about who "gets it."

Therefore the disciples in Matthew are not the dunces they are in Mark. Matthew's Jesus demands no less devotion than Mark's, but he requires less puzzling. To go back to the examples of the two houses, Jesus' reputation as a leader depends upon those who hear his words and act on them. Matthew is unwilling to have the disciples be ignorant hearers and tarnish Jesus' legacy. This gospel depends upon an unbroken transmission of teachings from Jesus to disciples to readers of Matthew. Since knowledge of Jesus' status as Lord (not teacher) stands as the ultimate goal for his readers, and since the disciples must transmit this knowledge, they understand Jesus quite well. They do so because, ultimately, Jesus' teaching depends on them.

In one exchange between Jesus and the disciples, Jesus hearkens back to a house built on the rock by explicitly connecting his identity with the disciples and their future disciples. In a scene drawn largely from Mark's gospel, Jesus quizzes the disciples about his identity:

> "But who do you say that I am?"
> Simon Peter answered, "You are the Messiah, the Son of the
>    living God."
> And Jesus answered him, "Blessed are you, Simon son of Jonah! For
> flesh and blood has not revealed this to you, but my Father in
> heaven. And I tell you, you are Peter, and on this rock I will build my
> church, and the gates of Hades will not prevail against it." (16:15–18)

Jesus makes a pun on Peter's name, which in Greek literally means "rock," but which also categorizes Peter as a wise man, who has heard and acted upon Jesus' words. The metaphorical enemy of the house on the rock (winds and rain) is now the gates of Hades, but in both cases the rock withstands the assault. Furthermore, Peter himself becomes the foundation for the church, which will build upon him, thus setting him and the other apostles as the intermediate material between Jesus and the readers of the gospel.

The earnestness of Matthew, however, can pose difficulties for modern interpreters. His narrative needs enemies in order to draw the protagonist and his disciples more sharply. Most often, the characters that play the role of builders on sand are Jewish authority figures. Matthew is absolutely certain that Judaism points to Jesus as its fulfillment; thus, to reject Jesus is to reject a correct understanding of Judaism. Matthew makes his case for Jesus as the fulfillment of Judaism in two ways. First, in order to prove that Jesus represents the apex of God's dealing with Jews, he begins his gospel with a genealogy that names Jesus as "son of David" and "son of Abraham," in the very first verse. These two characters of the Hebrew Bible received promises from God, and now Jesus becomes the fleshly heir to both. After establishing Jesus' family credentials, Matthew secondly argues from scriptural citation of the Hebrew Bible. Depending on how one counts, Matthew punctuates his narrative with ten to fifteen scripture references that demonstrate Jesus' continuity with the Hebrew scriptures. For example, in the story of the flight to Egypt, when Joseph, Mary, and Jesus flee the wrath of Herod, Matthew writes: "This was to fulfill what had been spoken by the Lord through the prophet, 'Out of Egypt I have called my son' " (2:15). Matthew's quotation of Hosea 11:1 here, along with the many other passages that he marshals as evidence, tries to convince the reader of the manifest connections between Jesus' life and the Hebrew Bible.

Many people within the gospel, not to mention later Jewish readers of Matthew, are not convinced. When it comes to portraying Jewish religious authorities, Matthew's surety and earnestness veer into polemic. Some of Jesus' most virulent statements in all the New Testament occur in Matthew 23, when

35

he harangues the Pharisees, calling them "hypocrites," "whitewashed tombs," and "blind guides." Before the crucifixion, the angry crowd cries out, "His blood be on us and on our children!" (27:25). It is important to recognize that Matthew's gospel in particular has been used for anti-Semitic purposes, largely due to its literary tendencies to present the world in black-and-white categories.

Matthew ends with a speech of Jesus, commonly known in Christian parlance as "The Great Commission": "Go therefore and make disciples of all nations, baptizing them in the name of the Father and of the Son and of the Holy Spirit, teaching them to obey everything that I have commanded you. And remember, I am with you always, even until the end of the age" (28:19–20). Just as Jesus' words were heard, believed, and acted upon by the disciples, they must now become the bearers of the words, encouraging more obedience and thus more disciples. If not for the faithful carrying forth of this commandment on the behalf of the disciples, Matthew's gospel does not get written. The gospel implicitly connects its own existence to the ability of the disciples to understand and pass on the teachings of Jesus. They will, it is assumed, make more disciples, who will separate themselves from those goats doomed to have their houses on the sand washed away.

## Luke-Acts

The Gospel of Luke and the book of Acts were written by the same author and together make up almost a quarter of the length of the New Testament canon. Apart from Paul's, Luke's voice stands as the most prominent among these writings. Most New Testament scholars read Luke and Acts together, using each as an aid to interpret the other. Oftentimes, the two-part work is hyphenated as Luke-Acts, as if it were one continuous work, the book of Acts picking up where the gospel leaves off. While the two books share stylistic traits as well as thematic concerns, it seems better to see Acts as a sequel to Luke rather than the second volume of a two-part work. There is no indication that Luke had Acts in mind when writing his gospel, and each stands as an independent work. To use an imperfect literary analogy, Luke is like *Tom Sawyer* and Acts like *Huckleberry Finn*. Both pairs of writings have overlapping characters and settings, but each book has its own aims understandable on its own terms. To use a counterexample, they are not like J. R. R. Tolkien's *Lord of the Rings*, in which each book of the trilogy cannot be read on its own terms.

## The Gospel of Luke

In one long elegant sentence, Luke's gospel begins with self-reflection:

> Since many have set their hands to arrange a narrative concerning the deeds that have been accomplished among us, just as the original eyewitnesses and ministers of the word handed them down to us, it also seemed good to me, since I have diligently followed all these things from the beginning, to write for you an orderly account, excellent Theophilus, in order that you might know the truth about the words you were taught. (1:1–4, author's translation)

Very succinctly, Luke presents a prehistory of his own work, his vision of the distinctive contributions of his own account, and the impetus for writing it. Alone among the gospel writers, he readily acknowledges his debt to other authors, and Mark is clearly one of the "many" who have set out to "arrange a narrative." Luke does not call into question the veracity of his literary forebears, but he finds them lacking; otherwise he would not be writing. His critique of the other writers turns on the words "narrative" and "orderly." What Luke implies in this opening—and what seems supported by the gospel and Acts—is that the previous documents he read, including Mark, lacked a clear narrative thread. To put it more bluntly, they lacked plot.

Luke pays close attention to plot and takes a long view of the scope of his story. In his portrayal of Jesus, he takes care to connect Jesus with the distant past of human history (his genealogy of Jesus goes all the way back to Adam [3:23–38]) and with the future existence of the church (mainly in Acts). Within the narrative itself, pieces often fit together in an intricate manner. For example, Jesus announces his mission in 4:16–30 and provokes the crowd to anger by comparing himself to Elijah and Elisha, two prophets from the Hebrew scriptures. These two prophets, in the episodes Jesus references, went outside Israel to perform miraculous deeds, Elijah resurrecting a widow's dead son and Elisha healing a Syrian soldier of leprosy. The crowd becomes incensed because Jesus seems to indicate a preference for Gentiles in his own work. Luke's insistence on an orderly account manifests itself later, when Jesus first heals a slave of a Roman soldier (7:1–10) and then raises the dead son of a widow (7:11–17). These two miracles mirror the examples Jesus provided in his pronouncement at the start of his public ministry. The truth of Jesus' self-proclamation as prophet to the Gentiles is borne out by his deeds. For Luke, prophecy needs fulfillment. This necessity relates to the last sentence of his prologue, in which he claims to write an orderly account so that "you might know the truth about the words you were taught." This claim implies that factual claims about Jesus lack sustainability without a clear narrative that threads those facts together. Certainty and order go hand in hand.

In this way Luke is, among the gospel writers, the most like a modern biographer. Unlike Mark's gospel, in which Jesus appears fully formed as an adult, Luke's gospel narrates not only Jesus' birth but also the events leading up to the birth, including an extended treatment of Jesus' mother, Mary. He devotes an entire chapter to Jesus' infancy and childhood, and in that chapter gives two frameworks for understanding his portrayal of Jesus. The first comes from the lips of an old man named Simeon, who holds the infant Jesus in his arms and pronounces Jesus to be "a light for revelation to the Gentiles and for glory to your people Israel" (2:32). At the end of the chapter Luke himself provides the summary statement, "The child grew and became strong, filled

The New Testament as Literature

38

with wisdom; and the favor of God was upon him" (2:40). To understand Luke's conception of Jesus means to understand the development of Jesus' character—as one who grows physically and mentally, and who builds bridges to both Jews and Gentiles.

The temperament of Luke's Jesus becomes most apparent when looking at the episodes unique to this gospel. These Lukan stories often emphasize compassion or a special concern for the downtrodden of society. Among the well-known stories particular to Luke are the visit of Gabriel to Mary, the announcement to the shepherds about Jesus' birth, the parables of the prodigal son and the good Samaritan, and the story of Jesus' visit with Zacchaeus. Most emphatically, at his crucifixion, Jesus' speech in Luke exemplifies his characterization in this gospel, by demonstrating his concern for those around him. On the way to the cross, he deflects pity from himself, saying "Daughters of Jerusalem, do not weep for me, but weep for yourselves and for your children" (23:28). On the cross itself, he asks for absolution for his tormenters with the famous statement, "Father, forgive them, for they do not know what they are doing" (23:34).[1] He then assures one of his fellow sufferers on the cross that both of them will be together in Paradise. Finally, his last statement, in sharp contrast to the anguished Jesus of Matthew and Mark who cries, "My God, my God, why have you forsaken me" (Matt. 27:46, Mark 15:34), Jesus resignedly states, "Father, into your hands I commend my spirit" (23:46). Among the gospel writers, Luke presents the most sympathetic and likable portrayal of Jesus. He exhibits a strong irenic quality in his characterization, highlighting those aspects of Jesus' words and deeds that are most appealing while downplaying antagonistic qualities.

The net literary effect of Luke's aesthetic choices is a gospel characterized by completeness. Not only is Luke's Jesus more congenial than Matthew's or Mark's, he is also more fully formed. In the same way that Luke gives Jesus a prehistory, he also ties up the loose ends of the story after the crucifixion. On the Sunday after his Friday execution, Jesus appears to two men who had fondly hoped that Jesus would be the Messiah and who now find themselves perplexed and despondent. Jesus does not immediately restore their hopes but rather explains his life story in the third person while concealing his true identity. Finally, after eating a meal with Jesus, the two men experience an epiphany: "Their eyes were opened and they recognized him, and he vanished from their sight. They said to each other, 'Were not our hearts burning within us while he was talking to us on the road, while he was opening the scripture to us?' " (24:31–32). It is not until the complete story of Jesus has been expounded that they understand their misplaced fears. These two men function as stand-ins for Luke's ideal reader, and they point to the necessity for his gospel. Jesus cannot be understood as a collection of facts; he needs narrative to make his truth comprehensible.

## Acts

The book of Acts begins very similarly to the gospel: "In the first book, Theophilus, I wrote about all that Jesus did and taught from the beginning until the day when he was taken up to heaven, after giving instructions through the Holy Spirit to the apostles whom he had chosen" (1:1–2). Although this statement explicitly looks backward to the gospel, it also asserts the primary focus of Acts— namely, the working of the Holy Spirit through the apostles. A few verses later, Luke allows Jesus himself to provide an explicit outline for the entire document. In 1:8, Jesus announces to his disciples "You will receive power when the Holy Spirit has come upon you; and you will be my witnesses in Jerusalem, in all Judea and Samaria, and to the ends of the earth." Like a well-constructed essay, the Acts precisely follows this prediction. In chapter 2, the apostles receive the Holy Spirit and perform miraculous, powerful deeds. After witnessing and gathering converts in Jerusalem (chaps. 3–7), they branch out into Judea and Samaria (chaps. 8–12). From chapter 13 until the end of the book, the focus turns to Paul, who eventually reaches Rome, which, as far as this narrative is concerned, is like reaching the ends of the earth.

The geographical outline of Acts, predicted by Jesus, commingles Luke's artistry with the rubric of a divine plan. As an author who makes his compositional role explicit, Luke is indebted to the literary genres of his milieu. He combines the adventure of the Greco-Roman novel with the details of Greco-Roman historical writing, and the result is the most entertaining composition of the New Testament. The tales embedded in Acts include excitements such as snakebite, fortune-telling, earthquakes, dreams and visions, a shipwreck, riots, an averted suicide, deadly parasitic worms, and numerous persons either struck dead or resurrected. Luke interweaves these crowd-pleasing stories with dates, locales, and historical personages in order to fulfill the duties of a historian. But lingering over the entirety of the book is Jesus' opening thesis statement, announcing that providence oversees the narrated events. While there is certainly suspense, drama, and even tragedy in Acts, the reader is always certain that the divine plan will prevail.

One way to see the central force at work in Acts is to ask who the protagonist of the book is. Obviously this is a moot question for the gospel, but it is an intriguing one for Acts. After the departure of Jesus in the first chapter, Luke's focus turns to Peter, who makes a rousing speech in chapter 2 and takes center stage until chapter 7. Then a newcomer, Stephen, dominates a pivotal scene that includes his martyrdom by stoning. Peter reappears in chapter 8, is pushed aside by two new characters (Philip and Saul) later in chapters 8 and 9, and then comes back to prominence in chapters 10–12. From then on, however, the narrative never leaves the side of Saul (now Paul), and Peter makes only one more token appearance (15:7). Acts ends somewhat abruptly with Paul under house arrest in Rome, "proclaiming the kingdom of God and teaching about the Lord Jesus Christ with all boldness and without hindrance" (28:31). The author declines to terminate the story of either Peter or Paul, and the hasty transference of attention from one to another makes neither of them an ideal candidate for the role of hero of the book.

The only character that pervades the book from start to finish is, in fact, the Holy Spirit. Although something of an impersonal force, the Holy Spirit displays all the literary accoutrements that a reader expects from a protagonist. We see the Spirit's "birth" (2:1–4), the deeds that the Spirit accomplishes (4:24–31), the Spirit's development and growth (10:44–48), and the interaction of the Spirit with other characters (15:28). The ending of Acts becomes less puzzling if we think of the book as the narrative of the expanding Holy Spirit, especially since Jesus' statement of 1:8 gives the maturation point of the Spirit as the ends of the earth, thus completing its mission (though not its existence, which is eternal).

A closer look at the speeches of the various characters of Acts reinforces the centrality of the Holy Spirit as character. One of the main devices Luke employs to propel his narrative is recounting public speeches. Often before the speech, he will describe the character as touched by the Holy Spirit. Compare the following statements:

> Then Peter, filled with the Holy Spirit, said to them . . . (4:8)

> But filled with the Holy Spirit, he [Stephen] gazed into heaven and saw the glory of God and Jesus standing at the right hand of God. "Look," he said . . . (7:55–56)

> But Saul, also known as Paul, filled with the Holy Spirit, looked intently at him and said . . . (13:9–10)

Whenever a character makes a speech, the Holy Spirit provides him his words. Thus the speeches sound remarkably similar in tone and content, allowing for some variation in the context of the speech. In reading the book of Acts, although the circumstances that various characters face differ, their reactions do not substantially change. To a great extent, Paul, Stephen, John, Paul, and Barnabas are interchangeable because since they all serve as mouthpieces for the same spirit, their personalities are swallowed up into a supernatural presence. That is why Luke does not bother completing their life stories. As individuals they have no meaning;

the characters in Acts are "good" only insofar as they allow
themselves to lose their distinct personae.

## Luke-Acts as a two-volume work

Each volume enlarges the scope of the other. Simeon's hope that
Jesus would be the light to the Gentiles is begun in Luke but truly
finds fruition in Acts. The domineering presence of the Holy
Spirit in Acts transpires only because Jesus gave up his spirit on
the cross and then ascended to heaven after his resurrection.
Most importantly, the presence of the sequel serves to bolster the
claims Luke makes in the gospel. Mark's and Matthew's works
leave the reader wondering about and perhaps doubting any
lasting legacy of Jesus. Luke writes Acts to remove any doubt
and to show that the historical life of Jesus continued to have
historical effects.

# John

Around the year 600 CE, Pope Gregory the Great was discussing
the varieties of biblical interpretation. He vividly described the
Bible as "almost like a river, both shallow and deep, in which a
lamb may walk and an elephant swim." Commentators on the New
Testament have often used Gregory's imagery to describe the
Gospel of John in particular. On the one hand, John would fit
comfortably into a primary school reader; when students are
learning Greek for the first time, they often begin with this gospel.
Yet, on the other hand, John stands as the most difficult of all the
gospels to understand conceptually. The first few verses of John
comprise a paradox of simplicity and complexity.

> In the beginning was the Word,
> And the Word was with God,
> And the Word was God.
> He was in the beginning with God.
> All things came into being through him,
> And without him not one thing came into being.

What has come into being in him was life,
And the life was the light of all people.
The light shines in the darkness,
And the darkness did not overcome it. (1:1–5)

Most ten-year-olds could easily read these words aloud,
understand the basic grammar, and make sense out of each line.
These children would be the lambs of Gregory's quotation. But an
interpretation of the verses as a whole goes beyond a ten-year-old's
capacity; this passage requires a complexity of thought more akin
to Gregory's elephants. All sorts of questions arise once we move
beyond the grammatical sense. How can the Word (and why is it
capitalized?) be with God while also being God? How did all things
come into being through the Word? What is the relationship
between light and life and why does the text move so quickly from
one noun to the next? All of these questions point to the necessity
of understanding John's gospel on a deeper, almost metaphysical
level.

William Blake is another poet who combines simplicity and
complexity in a similar manner to John. Many of his poems from
*Songs of Experience* and *Songs of Innocence* appear in anthologies
of children's verses and are memorized by very young children.
Lines like these from his poem "The Lamb" have much in common
with the prologue of John.

> Little lamb, who made thee?
> Dost thou know who made thee?
> Gave thee life and bid thee feed
> By the stream and o'er the mead;
> Gave thee clothing of delight,
> Softest clothing, woolly, bright;
> Gave thee such a tender voice,
> Making all the vales rejoice?
> Little Lamb, who made thee?
> Dost thou know who made thee?

Both Blake and John use short clauses, often repeating key words. With some exceptions, both authors employ simple vocabulary. But neither poet belongs solely in a children's collection; in disarmingly simple language, each provokes multiple interpretations that go well beyond a simplistic reading. Both poets tend to allow for a facile reading that later gains complexity, as a reader moves to maturity.

Unlike Blake's work, John's lines display very few features associated with lyric poetry. These first five verses, along with the rest of 1:1–18, appeal to the intellect rather than emotion, elevating concepts over imagery. The gospel begins not with a narrative but with this poetic prologue. Placed at the beginning of the gospel, this overture provides guidelines for understanding the prose narrative that will follow. In a series of metaphors, John associates the Word of verses 1–5 with not only life and light but also with flesh, specifically the flesh of Jesus, the only begotten of the Father. In a remarkably few verses, John combines these conceptual snapshots into a montage that the rest of the gospel will explore more fully. This beginning stands outside the main narrative, but it gives the reader a glossary for understanding it.

John's gospel, like the prologue, emphasizes such key words as "believe," "signs," "witness," and "son" that must be understood in order to make sense of the whole. Although none of the gospels is primarily plot-driven, in John the plot is subservient to conceptualization. Making sense of the story of John's gospel depends upon making sense of the vocabulary of John's gospel. This manner of presentation works on two levels. Within the narrative itself, Jesus essentially teaches vocabulary lessons to his hearers. His intention is to draw them into his own way of defining certain terms, and if they do so, they prove themselves to be ones who understand, or more accurately, ones who believe and thus can be called "children of God" (1:12). On a second level, the gospel presents its readers with the same challenge. At the end of gospel (before the epilogue of chapter 21), John writes, "These things are written so that you may come to believe that Jesus is the Messiah, the Son of God, and that through believing you may have life in his name" (20:31). Jesus' words, therefore, address not only the characters in the gospel but also the reader who looks over the shoulders of the characters. Both Jesus and John present a stark challenge: you must accept my own language, my own terminology in order to understand me. To hear me incorrectly and to read me wrongly demonstrates that you are not a child of God but rather a child of the devil (8:42–48).

Two conversations toward the beginning of John exemplify the two levels of Jesus' challenge. In both of these conversations, Jesus seems intent upon confounding the people who talk to him, even as they come to him for answers. First, a religious official named Nicodemus comes at night (perhaps because he is not part of the light?) to learn more about him. He addresses Jesus cordially, "Rabbi, we know that you are a teacher who has come from God, for no one can do these signs you do apart from the presence of God" (3:2). Ignoring the compliment, Jesus responds with a verbal challenge, which plays on the double meaning of the Greek word *anothen*, which can mean either "from above" or "again": "Very truly, I tell you, no one can see the kingdom of God without being born *anothen*" (3:3). Politely overlooking the fact that he had not asked about the kingdom of God, Nicodemus replies to this non sequitur by asking for clarification about being born a second time. Jesus disregards Nicodemus's response because it is incorrect: Jesus meant "from above," and Nicodemus heard "again." So Jesus shifts the discussion a second time by punning again, this time with the Greek word *pneuma*, which means spirit or breath: "The pneuma blows where it chooses, and you hear the sound of it, but you do not know where it comes from or where it goes. So it is with everyone who is born of the pneuma." This time Nicodemus does not bother to keep the dialogue going, so he asks in frustration, "How can these things be?" (3:9). Jesus responds with condescension: "Are you a teacher of Israel and yet you do not understand these things?" (3:10).

Jesus has deliberately thwarted Nicodemus's attempt to understand him. Throughout the conversation, he refuses to answer Nicodemus directly, consistently changing both topic and metaphor. Jesus continues to talk for the rest of the chapter, but by this point the dialogue has become a monologue. Nicodemus mysteriously disappears from the narrative after Jesus' belittling of him. He never receives understanding nor gets the opportunity to have his questions clarified. His original addressing of Jesus as rabbi (teacher) proves exceptionally ironic since Jesus never actually teaches but instead talks about himself.

The second example follows on the heels of the encounter with Nicodemus. In a dialogue with a Samaritan woman in chapter 4, Jesus begins by bluntly asking, "Give me a drink." When she comments on how strange it is that he, a Jewish man, initiates a conversation with her, a Samaritan woman, Jesus continues to talk about water, but he moves from talking about literal water to metaphorical water. After this metaphor reaches a dead end (due to the woman's reluctance to engage in metaphorical dialogue), he talks to the woman about her past marriages and then expounds on the various places that Jews and Samaritans worship. Finally, he ends with a clear claim to be the Messiah. Throughout this conversation and throughout the gospel, Jesus cannot stop talking about himself and, if the conversation begins to stray away from his concerns, he will forcefully pull it back. The difference between Nicodemus and the Samaritan woman is that she does not lose patience and has the tenacity to jump through the verbal hoops that Jesus pulls out. By the end of chapter 4, the Samaritan woman, along with many of her townspeople, believe in Jesus as the Messiah.

In both these episodes, Jesus emphasizes words. After the Word becomes flesh (1:14), the Word spawns words. In the conversations

47

with Nicodemus and the Samaritan woman, Jesus proffers special meanings for common words: spirit, worship, water, born, thirst. To engage in a dialogue with Jesus means letting him define words as he will. He becomes the master of language itself. He asserts this claim most forcefully in a dispute with the Pharisees:

> "I am going away, and you will search for me, but you will die in your sin. Where I am going, you cannot come." Then the Jews said, "Is he going to kill himself? Is that what he means by saying, 'Where I am going, you cannot come'?" He said to them, "You are from below, I am from above; you are of this world, I am not of this world. I told you that you would die in your sins, for you will die in your sins unless you believe that I am he." They said to him, "Who are you?" Jesus said to them, "Why do I speak to you at all?" (8:21–25)

Indeed, the reader must be asking the same question along with "Why do they bother speaking to him?" (Later his enemies will in fact ask, "Why listen to him?" [10:20]). Clearly no communication takes place between Jesus and his enemies. One way that speakers of English can gauge how well they are communicating is to ask, "Do you know where I'm coming from?" The idiom "coming from" does not have the same connotation in Greek, but the colloquialism certainly illustrates the failure of communicating in John. In the English question, the speaker implies that unless the hearer knows the origin of the speaker's stance, the hearer cannot understand. Jesus makes a similar claim when he says, "You are from below, I am from above (*anothen*)." This assertion echoes the prologue's opening verse, "The Word was with God." The gospel opens by saying that Jesus has come down from heaven. Three times in the gospel, Jesus' enemies discuss his origin. First they dismiss his claim to be the "bread from heaven" by asserting Joseph as his father (6:42). A second time they assert that he cannot possibly be the Messiah because no one will know where the Messiah comes from, and they know where he is from. (7:27) A third time, they assert the opposite—that they do *not* know where he comes from, and therefore his teachings are suspect (9:29). The characters who reject Jesus find themselves in a double bind. They certainly reject Jesus within the logic of the story, and he castigates them for not understanding his origin. Yet, in a sense, Jesus punishes his hearers for not having *read* the gospel itself. The readers of John's gospel have a distinct advantage over Jesus' foils because the beginning of the gospel explains Jesus' origin. Without this textual aid, and without the leisure to dwell upon the significance of the words of Jesus, the characters *within* the gospel become perplexed, befuddled, or exasperated.

John's gospel, consequently, makes less a narrative demand on the reader than it does a semantic one. Because John repeats specialized vocabulary he requires a circular reading, returning often to earlier places to rediscover meaning. For instance, in chapter 2, Jesus rids the temple of merchants and money-changers. As justification for his action, he says, "Take these things out of here! Stop making my Father's house a marketplace" (2:16). This provokes a confrontation with onlookers who question his actions. Jesus tells them that if the temple is destroyed he would "raise it up" in three days, an answer they scoff at. Then the narrator says, "But he was speaking of the temple of his body. After he was raised from the dead, his disciples remembered that he had said this" (2:21-22). John's explanation equates the physical temple, "my father's house," with the metaphorical temple of Jesus' body. In the context of this passage, this metaphor is simple enough, but the reader must recall it much later in the gospel, when Jesus addresses his disciples just before his death. In that conversation, he tries to comfort them:

> "Do not let your hearts be troubled. Believe in God, believe also in me. In my Father's house there are many dwelling places. If it were not so, would I have told you that I go to prepare a place for you? And if I go and prepare a place for you, I will come again and will take you to myself, so that where I am, there you may be also." (14:1-3)

Most readers understand this passage to indicate heaven. On the surface, such a meaning would seem obvious, but this gospel rarely lends itself to superficial readings. Jesus' own words, combined with John's narrative aside, emphatically equated "Father's house" with temple and with Jesus' body. When "Father's house" appears again in this later conversation, it carries with it the earlier definition. In the semantic web of John's gospel, Jesus points not heavenward but to the mystical sense that the disciples will dwell within his body. In chapter 15, he expounds on the future relationship between Father, Son, and disciples when he states, "Abide in me, as I abide in you" (15:4). The word "abide" is from the same root as "dwelling places." This seemingly straightforward statement about the afterlife proves to be layered with as much complexity as most passages in John.

John's gospel and John's Jesus, therefore, differ strikingly from the Synoptics. In terms of the narrative, John contains no parables, no birth stories, no exorcisms, no Eucharist scene, no temptation story. With regard to characterization, John's Jesus does not suffer like Mark's Jesus, rarely teaches like Matthew's Jesus, and has little concern for the marginalized as does Luke's Jesus. This gospel differs most from the Synoptics, however, by presenting the reader with a literary challenge. It provokes a decision about what words mean and about who provides words with their correct signification. Put a different way, the gospel leaves the reader with Pilate's question of 18:38: "What is truth?"

## Four ways of looking at Jesus

At the beginning of this chapter, I alluded to how the gospels might disappoint readers that want to uncover the historical Jesus. The gospel writers were not ruled by dispassionate objectivity; they created narratives. For those interested in the New Testament, their creativity must surely be considered an asset, not a liability. The gospels have a depth that reporting alone could never match. With the four gospels linked together at the beginning of the New Testament, four Jesuses, all intriguing and distinct yet overlapping, literary readers of these texts find an abundance of material that piques their own creative impulses.

# Chapter 4
# Paul and his letters

The great oddity of the New Testament is that the majority of its books are personal letters. Out of the twenty-seven books of the canon, at least twenty are pieces of correspondence (Hebrews and Revelation both have epistolary characteristics but are not letters per se), usually written to churches but sometimes to individuals. Reading these documents means looking over the shoulders of the original recipients to read their mail.

In this century, electronic communication—usually as curt as possible—has consigned the handwritten letter to near extinction. Yet in eras preceding ours, letter writers often crafted exquisite personal correspondence. Writers could even consult handbooks that outlined proper epistolary techniques, and they wrote leisurely and expansively. Intellectual figures envisioned that their letters might be published in the future, so the distinction between public correspondence and private was often obscured. Many examples from history exemplify the artistry of letter writing for posterity. In the famous correspondence of John Adams and Thomas Jefferson, both writers expected that their wide-ranging exchanges about religion and politics would eventually be read by others. One of the best-known literary concepts of John Keats occurs in a letter written to his brothers, expressing his admiration for Shakespeare's "negative capability," a quality he believed all poets should possess. This short letter has had a lasting impact upon literary theory. Similarly, Flannery O'Connor provided some of the best interpretation of her own short stories through her voluminous correspondence, now collected in a book-length anthology. Although letters have always contained personal and sometimes trivial information, they have often expressed scintillating insights of great figures.

Even a most cursory reading of the New Testament letters demonstrates that their authors employed rhetorical skill and thoughtfulness in their compositions. These letters are acts of purposeful rhetoric, not hasty memos. These writers attempted to persuade their audiences to accept certain viewpoints and to take certain actions. If we consider letter writing as conscious craft, the etymological similarity between "letter" and "literature" does not seem far-fetched.

## The importance of Paul

Paul stands as the preeminent letter writer of early Christian literature. Because of these epistles that were collected and codified, Paul has been enormously influential in the Western world. Such figures as Augustine and Luther drew their inspiration from Paul, and they would not have acquired their prominence without his inspiration. Paul has even wielded a lasting linguistic power. The English language has borrowed certain words from Paul—grace, faith, justification, atonement, redemption—and our understanding of such words is distinctively colored by his employment of them. Because Paul's writings have been absorbed into Western thought and because his writings have become so closely aligned with popular Christian theology, the details of his letters are often obscured by received wisdom. The task of a literary analysis of Paul differs somewhat from that of the gospels because the stereotypical questions about plot, conflict, and drama do not apply. Yet the method is the same; we still explore the contours of language itself. A literary reader of Paul must resist the temptation to construe him as an abstract thinker. Most New

Testament scholarship has tried to identify the center of his theology or, more hopelessly, the system of his thought. We will avoid that temptation and picture Paul as a persuader, a theologically imaginative pastor, and a passionate exponent of a particular worldview.

## Historical matters

Paul was a contemporary of Jesus but he never met him. We must guess at his birth year, but it seems reasonable to say he was born shortly after Jesus (ca. 10 CE), and tradition says that he died in Rome around the year 64 CE, when he was beheaded by Nero. He was born and reared in Tarsus, a cosmopolitan city off the northeastern Mediterranean coast. He spent his adult years traveling all around the eastern Mediterranean. Our knowledge about Paul's life comes both from his letters and from the book of Acts, though Luke's account of him does not always mesh with his own testimony.

Thirteen letters claim Paul as their author. Of these, the vast majority of scholars consider three of them—1 Timothy, 2 Timothy, and Titus—pseudonymous. According to this view, after Paul's death, one of his followers wrote these letters (usually called The Pastoral Epistles) in Paul's name, carrying forward Paul's legacy. A fair number of scholars also doubt that Paul wrote Ephesians, Colossians, and 2 Thessalonians. Although a literary analysis of Paul's letters does necessarily address historical questions, it is impossible to avoid a decision on which of Paul's letters to include here. I opt for a compromise. The Pastorals differ enough from the other letters that they will be ignored here. The other three disputed letters, however, have close enough affinities with the rest of the Pauline corpus to merit consideration. Thus the ten letters that form the basis of the following discussion are: Romans, 1 and 2 Corinthians, Galatians, Ephesians, Philippians, Colossians, 1 and 2 Thessalonians, and Philemon. The order they appear in the New Testament roughly corresponds to length and weightiness. Romans and 1 Corinthians each have sixteen chapters and often present very difficult arguments. These contrast sharply with Philemon, which is a short, one-chapter letter that encourages a slave-owner to take back a slave.

## Paul, audiences, rhetoric, and letters

When an author decides to write a letter, he or she creates a persona. The conventions that exist for writing letters—beginning the letter with an address, closing with some parting words—help establish the intended roles of sender and receiver. There is a formality in composing a long document sent to an audience (this word is ironic, since it relates to hearing) that does not exist in face-to-face conversation. A careful letter writer will craft the tone of the letter, its style, content, and structure in a manner that presents an authorial persona useful to the purposes at hand. The writer imagines the likely readers of the letter, contemplates their attitude toward the writer, decides the message to send, and then marshals the stylistic devices that will best enable communication. For a writer like Paul, of whom we have many letters, this means that each one will have unique features, depending on what he wants to emphasize. More specifically, the dynamics of letter writing make it clear that in each of his letters, Paul creates both a self-characterization and an audience creation.

I dwell on the dynamics of epistolary composition because too often scholars and readers talk about "Paul" as if they could map his personality directly from his letters. Every time Paul (or any letter writer) constructs a letter, however, he fictionalizes himself. This is not to say that Paul is dishonest or cynically manipulative; rather that he can control and bend the aspects of his personality he decides to reveal to his audiences. We should always remember that the Paul of the letters, just like Paul in Acts, is a literary character. He is, to be sure, a historical person as well, but we do not have the advantage of a modern biographer to construct "the real Paul," any more than we could discover the "real Jesus," as opposed to the literary character.

The same dynamics apply to the recipients of the letters as well. Most people read Paul as if he were talking to a generalized reader, but with letter writing, such a nonspecific reader does not exist. Clearly the original audiences were citizens of Galatia, Rome, and other locales in the ancient world. (The name of each letter refers to the geographical locale of the recipients; thus Galatians is written to Christians in the province of Galatia, Romans to residents of Rome). Literarily, Paul portrays an audience in each letter, an audience he imagines and creates, just as he creates himself.

As a writer of Greek, Paul necessarily employed Greek rhetoric (using the sense of rhetoric in the broad sense of communication). Although he was probably not trained as a classical rhetorician, he certainly developed impressive literary skills. Ancient Greek writers, Aristotle in particular, described three means of rhetorical persuasion: (1) ethos, which centered on the persuasive status of the speaker; (2) pathos, which appealed to the emotions of the audience; and (3) logos, which referred to the order and logic of the content. Ideally all three would work together to convince an audience of the speaker's message. With regard to Paul, since his letters have had so much theological influence, most readers have disproportionately explored the logos or content of his letters and tried to figure out what he meant. The other two aspects, however—ethos and pathos—prove just as intriguing. He seeks to define his authority (ethos) and to affect the emotions of his audiences (pathos), with the ultimate goal of conveying a certain message (logos).

This tripartite nature of persuasion proves especially useful in an analysis of letters. Written communication must include a writer, a recipient, and the letter itself. Understanding the dynamics of correspondence necessitates exploring all three elements. In what follows, I employ the categories of ethos, pathos, and logos as a means to discuss Paul's persona, his construction of an audience, and the content of his writing.

# Ethos—the character of Paul

To demonstrate how difficult it might be to historicize Paul through his letters, consider this thought experiment. Suppose you were to find in a trunk a large collection of letters your great-grandmother had written. Assume also that you knew very little about her life except for those letters. The letters in the trunk have multiple audiences, including her children, her husband, the farm bureau, a class of fourth graders, her close friend, and her parents. She may or may not choose to give many details about her personal life, depending on her audience. As a reader, you would have to discern how self-disclosing or aloof she was in the writings you perused. Undoubtedly, the picture you gather from your reading would differ greatly from that of a close friend of hers. It is important to note that neither the character gleaned from the letters nor the one given by her friend represents the "true self." Characterization *is* interpretation, and to claim that Paul is a literary character means no more or less than taking the evidence he presents and drawing inferences and conclusions about it.

The character of Jesus is developed through third-person narration. Although the gospel writers occasionally peer into Jesus' mind to explain what he was thinking, they primarily characterize him through speech and actions, with little narrative explanation. For Paul, the opposite is true. What we glean about his character comes either from self-reflective accounts or from his understanding of others' characterization. He gives few autobiographical details in his letters. Much of what we can say about his historical life comes from reading between the lines and filling in details from the book of Acts. Yet the character of Paul blazes brighter than Jesus' because it confronts the reader in almost every verse. As a character, Paul displays such a rich variety of moods and temperaments—alternatively despairing and joyful, consoling and chastising, humble and overbearing—that makes it difficult to caricature him.

Unfortunately, he has, in fact, been subject to various caricatures—the heavy-handed inventor of Christianity, a hateful or self-indulgent paranoiac, an ardent misogynist, and the proclaimer of grace by faith. All of these generalizations reduce Paul to a singular type and thereby overlook what one New Testament scholar has called Paul's protean nature. The advantage of a literary reading of Paul is that it allows for depth and contradiction, in a manner that a systematic reading of Paul does not. A literary investigation of Paul's letters does not primarily attempt to explain Paul's theology. Neither does a literary reading present a psychoanalytic or historical portrait of Paul. It begins, rather, with Paul's self-characterization.

## Autobiographical details

Something dramatic happened to Paul, and this religious encounter becomes the starting point for what he calls "the gospel." In his letter to the Galatians, Paul gives more autobiographical information than anywhere else, but even here, he provides only a brief sketch.

> You have heard, no doubt, of my earlier life in Judaism. I was violently persecuting the church of God and was trying to destroy it. I advanced in Judaism beyond many among my people of the same age, for I was far more zealous for the traditions of my ancestors. But when God, who had set me apart before I was born and called me through his grace, was pleased to reveal his Son to me, so that I might proclaim him among the Gentiles ... I went away at once into Arabia, and afterwards I returned to Damascus.
> Then after three years ... I was still unknown by sight to the churches of Judea that are in Christ; they only heard it said, "The one who formerly was persecuting us is now proclaiming the faith he once tried to destroy." And they glorified God because of me. (Gal. 1:13–24)

Paul tells his story in a three-part stage to the Galatian church. First he describes his actions before God's revelation to him. With no small degree of confidence, Paul admits his zeal for Judaism, manifested in his "persecuting the Church of God and trying to destroy it." Second, he receives a revelation from God that impels him to "proclaim" among the Gentiles. For some reason, untold to his audience, this revelation results in a sojourn of some indefinite period. The third stage in Paul's self-narrative shifts toward the proclamation itself, summed up in the anonymous report about him, where those who heard of his conversion "glorified God" because of this new Paul.

This brief narrative closely resembles what Paul says about himself in Philippians 3:4b–9a:

> If anyone else has reason to be confident in the flesh, I have more: circumcised on the eighth day, a member of the people of Israel, of the tribe of Benjamin, a Hebrew born of Hebrews; as to the law, a Pharisee; as to zeal, a persecutor of the church; as to righteousness under the law, blameless.
>
> Yet whatever gains I had, these I have come to regard as loss because of Christ. More than that, I regard everything as loss because of the surpassing value of knowing Christ Jesus my Lord. For his sake I have suffered the loss of all things, and I regard them as rubbish, in order that I may gain Christ and be found in him. (Phil. 3:4b–9a)

These verses in Philippians, like those in Galatians, narrate a life divided into a before-Christ and an after-Christ period. In his before-Christ period, Paul conducted an exemplary life as a Pharisaic Jew. Nothing in Paul's letters betrays any sense of inadequacy he felt during this period; he was completely confident that his life in Judaism pleased God. Only in his after-Christ period did Paul express any critique for his life as a Pharisee, and even then, it seems less a critique than a realization of that old life's meagerness for him. In this after-Christ period, Paul remains thoroughly Jewish and committed to Judaism, but he has reconfigured what the word *Judaism* means. It now includes adherence to the God of Israel *and* to Jesus, who has paved the way for both Israel and for Gentiles to be part of God's people.

While he provides a few other tidbits of autobiographical information, especially at the closings of his letters when he talks about travel plans (cf. Rom. 16 and 1 Cor. 16), what he narrates most often is his experience of persecution. Especially in 2 Corinthians he emphasizes his sufferings, at one point cataloguing all the various physical torments he has had to endure. The long list seems like an extreme case of "woe is me":

> Five times I have received from the Jews the forty lashes minus one.
> Three times I was beaten with rods. Once I received a stoning. Three
> times I was shipwrecked; for a night and a day I was adrift at sea; on
> frequent journeys, in danger from rivers, danger from bandits,
> danger from my own people, danger from Gentiles, danger in the
> city, danger in the wilderness, danger at sea, danger from false
> brothers and sisters; in toil and hardship, through many a sleepless
> night, hungry and thirsty, often without food, cold and naked.
> And, besides other things, I am under daily pressure because of my
> anxiety for all the churches. Who is weak, and I am not weak?
> (2 Cor. 11:24–29a)

On its own, this may sound like an old man's complaint about how terrible his life is in order to gain sympathy from his readers. But in the context of this letter, Paul provides this litany not to draw pity but admiration. He is convinced that unless a person undergoes a certain bout of hardship, that person must not be a follower of Christ. Paul thinks that his own experience replicates much of what Jesus underwent. In a succinct and bold statement, he says, "Be imitators of me, as I am of Christ" (1 Cor. 11:1). The way in which an outside observer might see him as an imitator of Christ is through his sufferings. In multiple places in his letters, he makes explicit the connection between his patterning of his life after Jesus and the sufferings he undergoes (e.g., Phil. 3:10, Col. 1:24).

## Paul's persona

As the previous passage demonstrates, Paul interprets his character through self-description more often than he narrates the actual events of his life. One of the clearest examples of his self-description appears in 1 Corinthians. This letter attempts to solve particularly divisive issues within the Christian community at Corinth by emphasizing unity. In the middle of a discussion about whether believers should assert their Christ-given rights, Paul states,

> For though I am free with respect to all, I have made myself a slave to all, so that I might win more of them. To the Jews I became as a Jew, in order to win Jews. To those under the law I became as one under the law (though I myself am not under the law) so that I might win those under the law. To those outside the law I became as one outside the law (though I am not free from God's law but am under Christ's law) that I might win those outside the law. To the weak I became weak, so that I might win the weak. I have become all things to all people, that I might by all means save some. I do it all for the sake of the gospel, that I may share in its blessings. (1 Cor. 9:19–23)

In the context of the letter, he is arguing that an emphasis on individual rights and freedom will prove destructive to the church. In a vivid metaphor, he urges the Corinthian congregation to think of themselves as a body. His own denial of his rights serves as an exemplar to the Corinthians, one that will alleviate their contentiousness. If every member of the congregation would subordinate his or her desires to the good of the whole church and to the furtherance of the gospel message, then disunity and dissention would be abolished. Paul utilizes the body metaphor to argue how silly it would be to assert individual rights: "The eye cannot say to the hand, 'I have no need of you,' nor again the head to the feet, 'I have no need of you'" (1 Cor. 12:21).

With regard to Paul himself, these few lines demonstrate Paul's distinctly pragmatic tendencies. He gladly and forthrightly acknowledges that he changes masks, depending on his interlocutors. The irony of exploring the character of Paul in his letters is that, by his own admission, this character will self-consciously be altered, according to his audience. When speaking to Jews, he asserts his Jewishness; when in contact with Gentiles, he downplays his Jewish identity. Notice, however, that there is a grounding factor—the gospel itself. When he uses the word *gospel*, he means something quite different from the New Testament genre; he indicates the entirety of the new understanding of God that stems from the life, death, and resurrection of Jesus. Paul considers this message to be paramount, and his biography becomes important to his addressees only insofar as it can illuminate and interpret that message. He can be completely flexible as long as the essentials of the gospel message are not being distorted. Once he sees that they are, however, he will muster any argument he can and will take on whatever role is necessary to see that such distortion is squashed.

In a remarkable sentence, he carries his pragmatic sensibilities almost to the point of supporting charlatans:

> Some proclaim Christ from envy and rivalry, but others from goodwill. These proclaim Christ out of love, knowing that I have been put here for the defense of the gospel; the others proclaim Christ out of selfish ambition, not sincerely but intending to increase my suffering in my imprisonment. What does it matter? Just this, that Christ is proclaimed in every way, whether out of false motive or true; and in that I rejoice. (Phil. 1:15–18)

In our age, where sincerity is highly valued and where religious figures whose words clash with their actions are vilified for hypocrisy, Paul's assertion here is jarring. He completely divorces motives from message. Yet in another passage, he presents a dissimilar attitude:

> For our appeal does not spring from deceit or impure motives or trickery, but just as we have been approved by God to be entrusted with the message of the gospel, even so we speak, not to please mortals, but to please God who tests our hearts. (1 Thess. 2:3–4)

How might these two contradictory claims about the relationship between motives and speech be reconciled? In both cases Paul is working out the dynamic between messenger and message. He intimates in his letter to the Thessalonians that they themselves correlate the speaker with the speech. In their minds, as Paul understands them, they need assurance of the reliability of the bearer of the gospel. Thus Paul assures them that his pure motives correspond to the pure gospel story. This is an implicit claim about the audience as well. They cannot believe the message without also believing in the messenger, so Paul reassures them that each reinforces the other. In the case of the Philippians, Paul is talking about a situation at a distance, where message and messenger do not seem so closely tied together. In that case, he clearly assumes that the message does *not* depend on the purity of the messenger. The guiding principle at work for Paul is not an abstract praise of sincerity but a dogged resolve to have the gospel message proclaimed. If the proclamation can remain pure in spite of the proclaimer, that's fine with Paul. If, however, the proclamation becomes *dependent* upon the status of the proclaimer, then purity and sincerity are necessary.

In many of Paul's letters, his audience connects the truth of the gospel with Paul's authority. In these cases Paul seems quite authoritarian. Toward the end of 2 Corinthians, in a particularly contentious section, he sounds threatening: "So I write these things while I am away from you, so that when I come, I may not have to be severe in using the authority that the Lord has given me for building up and not for tearing down" (13:10). But in other letters, where his own character is not an issue, Paul does not assert his authority at all. In one letter, Philemon, he does both. In this brief letter, Paul urges a person named Philemon to take back his slave Onesimus, who has become a valued companion of Paul while he was in prison. Paul uses both the carrot and the stick to convince Philemon:

> though I am bold enough in Christ to command you to do your duty, yet I would rather appeal to you on the basis of love.... I wanted to keep him with me..., but I preferred to do nothing without your consent, in order that your good deed might be voluntary and not something forced.... So if you consider me your partner, welcome him as you would welcome me.... I say nothing about your owing me even your own self.... Confident of your obedience, I am writing to you, knowing that you will do even more than I say. One thing more—prepare a guest room for me. (Phlm. 8–22, selections)

The way Paul oscillates between appealing to Philemon's generosity and issuing a vaguely stern command to take Onesimus back seems almost comic. He feels certain that his friendly admonition will be effective, but he reserves the right to become more forceful if necessary. He also assumes that Philemon will respect both his gentle recommendation and his absolute demand, if it comes to that. Paul calls himself a father in this letter, and he plays the role of both the encouraging, loving parent and the occasionally harsh parent.

So throughout his letters, Paul's persona shifts according to both audience and subject matter. His personality, if we wish to use that word, is quite difficult to pin down. This is not to say that he is a charlatan devoted to expediency alone. By any charitable reading, Paul cares deeply for his addressees. Sometimes that care comes across as care for his own authority, but the caricature of him as a selfish martinet cannot be sustained. To use an oxymoronic tag, Paul should be labeled as a flexible ideologue. His life and persona are intricately tied up with his message, but the message is supreme. His persona molds itself into a shape that complements the message.

## Logos—the gospel message and salvation

> For I am not ashamed of the gospel; it is the power of God
> for salvation to everyone who has faith, to the Jew first and
> also to the Greek. (Rom. 1:16)

Paul's negative statement at the beginning of Romans attributes a
capacious meaning to the word *gospel*. As we saw earlier, Paul does
not know of the literary genre of gospel, and he probably has very
limited information about Jesus. He rarely quotes Jesus (1 Cor.
11:24) and gives no indication that he knows much about Jesus'
public activity. His letters predate any other Christian texts, and
he certainly does not have access to the abundance of stories that
Mark or John did. When Paul refers to gospel, he means both
the minimally constructed narrative of Jesus' life, death, and
resurrection, and the theological significance of that narrative.
The gospel here serves as the object of many verbs in Paul's
letters; it is something that can be entrusted, distorted, preached,
received, heard, confirmed, confessed, and ministered. To
understand how Paul uses *gospel* and *salvation* provides an
excellent starting point for understanding Paul's message—the
logos of his communication.

Because Paul believes that his gospel can provide "salvation for
everyone who believes," he claims to have insight into the universal
predicament of all humans. The use of the word *salvation* makes
sense only if humans need to be saved from something. One of the
most famous interpreters of Paul, Martin Luther, read the
following passage from Romans 7 and found in it the root problem
of human beings:

> I do not understand my own actions. For I do not do what I want,
> but I do the very thing I hate. Now if I do what I do not want, I
> agree that the law is good. But in fact it is no longer I that do it, but
> sin that dwells within me. For I know that nothing good dwells
> within me, that is, in my flesh. I can will what is right, but I cannot

do it. For I do not do the good I want, but the evil I do not want is what I do.

For I delight in the law of God in my inmost self, but I see in my members another law at war with the law of my mind, making me captive to the law of sin that dwells in my members. Wretched man that I am! Who will rescue me from this body of death? Thanks be to God through Jesus Christ our Lord!

So then, with my mind I am a slave to the law of God, but with my flesh I am a slave to the law of sin. (Rom. 7:15–25)

Readers can rarely keep from sympathizing with Paul here as he portrays the lack of willpower that is endemic to human frailty. He seems to describe perfectly everyone's failed New Year's resolutions or susceptibility to temptation. Luther, who throughout his life experienced internal struggle, saw in Romans 7 the lifelong battle between flesh and spirit that every human experiences. Based on his reading, Luther considered a Christian to be *simul justus et peccator*, a Latin phrase that means "at the same time a sinner and justified."

Luther was wrong. He underestimated Paul's ability to present his message by means of a fictitious "I." Paul seduces the reader here into sympathizing with a fictional persona. If we compare Romans 7 to other places where Paul speaks in the first person, it becomes apparent that he would never say of himself "wretched man that I am." He might admit he once was wretched, but having experienced the grace of God, Paul's wretchedness, if it ever existed at all, has been obliterated. The language in the rest of Romans exposes how untenable Luther's reading is:

We know that our old self was crucified with him so that the body of sin might be destroyed, and we might no longer be enslaved to sin. (Rom. 6:6)

So you also must consider yourselves dead to sin and alive to God in Christ Jesus. (Rom. 6:11)

Here, Paul emphatically claims that sin no longer has power over those who have faith in Christ, a claim which refutes Luther's interpretation. In other words, the all-too-human dilemma of Romans 7 portrays the struggle that people have who have *not yet* come to faith in Christ. The rhetorical flourishes of these verses further point to their fictive nature. Paul infuses the lines with a comic sarcasm through the repetition of "do" and "do not." Especially if it is read aloud, the "I" seems not only morally anguished but pathetically confused and paralyzed by immature indecision. This type of character precisely represents what God has come to fix.

Luther's reading, repeated by many others, does not do justice to the depth and artistry of Paul. People read Romans 7 the way that some read Robert Frost's "The Road Not Taken." That poem closes with a famous stanza:

> I shall be telling this with a sigh
> Somewhere ages and ages hence:
> Two roads diverged in a wood, and I—
> I took the one less traveled by,
> And that has made all the difference.

Innumerable high school valedictory addresses have quoted that poem as an homage to individual choice and freedom that ends triumphantly. Such a reading works only if one glosses over the word "sigh," which indicates resignation if not regret, and if one forgets that the poet has claimed that the two roads in actuality were "about the same." Frost himself described the poem as "tricky," and almost all close readings of this poem see it falling well short of vibrant individualism. Paul's chapter in Romans seems just as tricky but also just as obviously ambiguous.

To read Romans 7 with its artfulness intact is to experience both the skill of Paul's rhetoric and the enormity of his existential claim. He entices his readers to empathize with the "I" of 7:14–25, but to empathize too completely would cause them to abandon their experience of salvation. Throughout Romans, Paul has developed a bond with his audience through the use of first person plural verbs ("we have received grace" [1:5], "we are justified by faith" [5:1], "we too might walk in newness of life" [6:4]). He wants them to agree with him that their lives have been irrevocably changed by faith and that sin no longer has power over them. The forceful appearance of the first person singular in 7:14–25 is therefore jarring, not only because it shifts from plural to singular but also because "I" now claims a dilemma that Paul has said "we" overcame. To read the "I" as an empathetic figure is tantamount to pulling oneself away from the "we" that has bound the reader with Paul. To put it another way, Paul wants the readers to put themselves in the place of the fictional "I," but then to realize that they are not that "I" any longer. Luther made the identification but then did not withdraw from it. The rhetoric of chapter 7 tests the reader's attentiveness to the previous chapter and asks, "Were you really listening?" On the flip side, it presents an "I" that both Paul and his audience can be glad to be rid of.

Throughout Paul's letters, he tells what he believes to be a universal story of humanity. It has both a historical and an existential dimension. Historically, he focuses on two distinct points. First, he trusts that the story of Adam and Eve accurately describes the way Sin taints the world. Human frailty and lack of trust in God resulted in failure. He talks of Adam as the one through whom Sin entered the world and because of Adam, following the story of Genesis, all humans experience death and decay (Rom. 5). Secondly, "in the fullness of time" (Gal. 4:4) Jesus came into the world to undo that which Adam had accomplished, Paul claims. Adam represents Sin and Death, Jesus is associated with sinlessless and eternal life. He does not think of these two characters as myths particular to Judaism; they are significant for all of humanity, even if individual humans do not know it.

Existentially this means that all humans, in the aftermath of Adam, are slaves to sin. This is not a choice; it is simply unavoidable.

Salvation, therefore, involves release from this slavery. Traditionally and popularly, Christian salvation involves avoidance of hell and the promise of heaven in the afterlife. While Paul clearly believes in an afterlife in heaven, he never mentions hell or eternal punishment. He only claims that "the unrighteous will not inherit the kingdom of God" (1 Cor. 6:9). He does not argue explicitly for universal salvation, but given his cocksureness about the universal human plight, he might very well claim that God will eventually save everyone. More pertinently, though, Paul's understanding of salvation has at least an equal if not a greater focus on what salvation means in the earthly existence of his audience.

Paul never shrinks from making grandiose claims about the effects of Christian conversion. To use an overworn cliché, Paul views Christianity as a life-changing experience, and his letters are filled with assertions that contrast between what once was and what now is. In Ephesians he summarizes the pattern of conversion that all Christians follow:

> You were dead through the trespasses and sins in which you once lived.... All of us once lived among them in the passions of our flesh, following the desires of flesh and senses, and we were by nature children of wrath, like everyone else. But God, who is rich in mercy, out of the great love with which he loved us even when we were dead through our trespasses, made us alive together with Christ—by grace you have been saved—and raised us up with him and seated us with him in the heavenly places in Christ Jesus. (Eph. 2:1–6)

This passage explains the intersection of the human story with Jesus' story. It is a connection that Paul makes over and over again (in, among other letters, Philippians, 1 Corinthians, and Galatians). As in a hymn in Philippians 2, Jesus came to earth from heaven, lived, died, and was resurrected. For Paul this is a complete and coherent encapsulation of Jesus' life; the details found later in the New Testament gospels are unimportant for Paul's narrative.

Above all, Paul highlights that Jesus conquered Death (he tends to personify it) through his resurrection. He takes this story of Jesus and makes it a microcosm for the story of human history. When he says to the Ephesians that "you were dead," this corresponds to Jesus' crucifixion. But because of the resurrection, God "raised us up with him." Jesus passed from death into life so that humanity might also pass from death into life. The mechanics of how humans participate in Jesus death and resurrection become complex as Paul discusses faith, justification, and atonement, but to a great extent those mechanics are secondary. The experience of salvation remains primary.

The universality of the gospel, the "good news" that Paul preaches to all people, however, can be polarizing as well as welcoming. While the gospel provides freedom for *all* people, it also is the *only* pathway to such freedom. He combines universality with exclusivity; Paul would not, like a good religious pluralist, claim that many paths lead to God. To be clear, Paul does not say that those who reject Jesus will be damned; in fact, he does not talk much about those who reject Jesus. He rather believes that those who do not have the faith of Jesus will continue to live as slaves of sin, in the dull deadness of the "passions of the flesh."

Depending on which pole of salvation is emphasized—the ignorant despair of the unsaved or the glorious union of the saved with God—Paul's rhetoric can sound rapturous or vitriolic. In 1 Corinthians 13 and Romans 8, he composes what verges on lyric poetry:

> If I speak in the tongues of mortals and of angels, but do not have love, I am a noisy gong or a clanging cymbal. And if I have prophetic powers and understand all mysteries and all knowledge, and if I have all faith, so as to remove mountains, but do not have love, I am nothing.... Love is patient; love is kind; love is not envious or boastful or arrogant or rude ... It bears all things, believes all things, hopes all things, endures all things. (1 Cor. 13:1–7)

> For I am convinced that neither death, nor life, nor angels, nor
> rulers, nor things present, nor things to come, nor powers, nor
> height, nor depth, nor anything else in all creation, will be able to
> separate us from the love of God in Christ Jesus our Lord. (Rom.
> 8:38–39)

These passages transcend theological disputations and
demonstrate that Paul is not primarily an abstract theologian.
A preoccupation with the propositional content of Paul's letters
dodges the visceral effects of Paul's writing in passages like these.
Here Paul lyrically relates the content of the salvation he explains
more propositionally elsewhere in Romans and Corinthians.

But other passages present the more exclusive and less attractive
side of Paul's message. In 2 Corinthians, he has been the subject of
a critique from others who are preaching the Christian message.
He thinks the Corinthian opponents have impugned the gospel, so
he goes on the defensive and the offensive at the same time. In an
ironic defense posture, he raves "like a madman" in recounting
credentials he thinks are unimportant (11:23). Taking the offense,
he attacks with bellicose language: "We destroy arguments and
every proud obstacle raised up against the knowledge of God, and
we take every thought captive to obey Christ. We are ready to
punish every disobedience when your obedience is complete"
(10:5–6). In this quest to destroy arguments, he sarcastically calls
his opponents the "super apostles," and presents them as bullies. In
passages like these, Paul refuses to brook any disagreement.

The combative pronouncements that ring from Paul's letters led
Friedrich Nietzsche to compose this scathing condemnation: "His
need was for power; ... Paul the priest wanted power once again—
he could use only concepts, doctrines, symbols with which one
tyrannizes masses and forms herds."[1] While Nietzsche may
represent an extreme distaste for Paul's arrogance, countless others
have been more than a little put off by Paul's hubris. This
description of Paul's desire for power, however, assumes Paul

wanted to set up a system in which he could dictate rules. Paul's message proclaims a universal salvation, but not systematically. It does not lack confidence, but neither does it primarily set forth doctrines. Strange as it may sound, Paul's message exhibits more naïveté than tyranny. His conception of salvation—distinctly colored by his personal experience—was so capacious that he could not understand why anyone would not accept it as eagerly as he had. He certainly does want people to follow his example, but not so much that he will be a dictator that "forms herds." Salvation in Paul's letters gleefully announces itself as the good news for everyone. It is a proclamation certain of its truth—so certain that it seems blissfully ignorant of the possibility that anyone might consider it unattractive.

## Pathos—Paul's audiences

In the communication that transpired between Paul and Christian churches, only Paul's voice has survived. Paul talks about letters he received back from churches, especially in the two Corinthian letters, but for the most part his recipients remain hazy reconstructions. It would be of great historical value to know the viewpoints of those whom he argued against and those he tried to cajole, but those voices have been lost to history.

In a close reading of the letters themselves, though, we can gain insight into his rhetorical construction of them. He often makes very personal appeals—the pathos of Greek rhetoric—in order to effect a change. Each letter fashions a recipient, and even though we do not hear the addressees speaking, Paul certainly characterizes them. A statistical analysis shows that Paul uses second person verbs (either singular or plural) almost seven hundred times in these ten letters. Such frequent use of "you" is astounding, even in personal missives. The vast majority of these verbs are second person plural ("you all"), indicating how centrally Paul values the communal aspect of his interaction with his readers.

Just as Paul can shape his own persona, so too he can portray his audience in a myriad of roles. The emotional distance between Paul and his audiences varies considerably among the writings. In Romans and Ephesians, he gives few clues about the hearers, and these letters keep the addressee at a formal distance. Philemon and Philippians both appeal to the loving bond between Paul and his correspondents. Other letters characterize the addressees with other images: recalcitrant children, argumentative competitors, fellow sufferers. The important point to remember about Paul's literary construal of the audiences is that he chooses the construal in order to present a message. It would be incorrect to suppose that Paul did not give just as much care to the language of address as he did to the language of theology. Thus, whether he writes with exasperation or flattery, he does so with pragmatic intent.

For more than half the letter of 1 Thessalonians, Paul expounds on his relationship with this congregation. In the first three (out of five) chapters, Paul uses first and second person pronouns (I, we, and you) for the subject of almost every single sentence. About himself and his co-writers, Silvanus and Timothy, he asserts their absolute honesty, their desire to see the Thessalonians, and their love for the recipients of this letter. In a striking metaphor, he reminds them: "But we were gentle among you, like a nurse tenderly caring for her own children. So deeply do we care for you that we are determined to share with you not only the gospel of God but also our own selves, because you have become very dear to us" (2:7–8). These verses construe both author and audience at the same time. While Paul presents himself as an extraordinarily caring person with maternal instincts, he also sets up the audience as children who receive lavish affection. He mixes the metaphor later, while still keeping familial language, when he says "we were made orphans by being separated from you" (2:17).

Such language creates an intimate trust between Paul and the Thessalonians. Paul presents himself as a trustworthy speaker who chooses to write for their welfare. The selflessness of a nurse caring for children, giving them medicine for curing or food for nourishment, corresponds to Paul's altruistic motives. Thus, when he moves toward providing instruction in chapters 4–5, he has set up a bond that allows such message to be accepted eagerly by his children.

The sequel, 2 Thessalonians, continues to emphasize the bond between the church and Paul. Although the first letter seems to have been misunderstood by some of the Thessalonians, Paul refrains from showing any irritation. He instead reiterates his pride in their actions:

> We must always give thanks to God for you, brothers and sisters, as is right, because your faith is growing abundantly, and the love of everyone of you for one another is increasing. Therefore we ourselves boast of you among the churches of God for your steadfastness and faith during all your persecutions and the afflictions that you are enduring. (2 Thess. 1:3–4)

When he does correct them, he still seems gentle as a nurse. Once he uses the phrase "we command you" (3:6), but then softens it by saying, "Do not be weary in doing what is right" (3:13). An earlier entreaty reads "we beg you" (2:1), a clear indication that he wants to establish a rapport with them, not a severe hierarchical relationship.

When Paul writes to the Galatians, he presents both himself and his audience in a diametrically opposed manner to the Thessalonian interchange. Most of his letters begin with a prayer of thanksgiving for his audience. Galatians skips this altogether and instead begins with dismay: "I am astonished that you are so quickly deserting the one who called you in the grace of Christ and are turning to a different gospel" (1:6). If in 1 Thessalonians Paul strived for intimacy, here in Galatians he seems determined to isolate himself. His language moves from ridicule ("You foolish Galatians! Who has bewitched you?" [3:1]) to acrid vulgarity

("I wish those who unsettle you would castrate themselves!" [5:12]). The Greek language does not include exclamation points, but the English punctuation captures the emphatic tone nicely. Throughout Galatians, Paul does not draw his audience toward him as he did in 1 Thessalonians, but rather dissociates himself by pushing them away. As he repeatedly states in his self-introduction, his calling from God did not depend on any other human being at all, much less on their approval.

This strident voice of Paul assumes that, by isolating himself, he can convince the Galatians that they are engaging in incorrect practices. Reading between the lines of this letter, the Galatians have started to practice rituals associated with Judaism, especially circumcision. When Paul wishes that the agitators would castrate themselves, he sarcastically points to this practice, as if to say, "If they are so fond of genital mutilation, why don't they go all the way?" In this letter, Paul does not view gentility as a useful mode of speech. Galatians is much more like a shouting match. Since certain people have convinced the Galatians to act differently from what they originally learned, Paul has to make his own voice heard. Furthermore, he paradoxically argues that his voice has greater authority *because* no one else agrees with him. He pictures the Galatians as noncompliant children that need a lecture, not encouragement.

Paul's "likeability," for lack of a better word, depends greatly on the construal of his audience. If the only letters of Paul that survived were Philippians, Thessalonians, and Romans, it seems doubtful that writers like Nietzsche would have such a negative opinion of him. Paul's unflattering portraits of the misguided recipients of Galatians and 2 Corinthians contribute greatly to unflattering portraits of Paul. The variety of audiences that Paul creates in his letters, however, warns against making blanket statements about Paul's relationship with them. Just as the author Paul differs from the historical Paul, it is equally true that the recipients of the letter are who Paul constructs them to be, not exactly the same as historical citizens living in Rome, Corinth, or Colossae. To read the letters well means to imagine the intended readers of the letter as Paul portrayed them and also imagine ourselves as that intended audience.

## Conclusion

Reading Paul's letters raises a host of questions about their effects on their original audiences. Did the Galatians react well to Paul's chastisement? Did Philemon take Onesimus back? Why did the Corinthians decide (if they were the ones who did) to keep and copy letters that were so critical of them? Answers to those questions are lost in time. The question for a contemporary literary reading of Paul is whether his letters still have an effect and, if so, on whom? Unlike the gospels, which are widely read by people who have no concern for religious questions, Paul's letters function almost exclusively within Christian communities. He has been held captive, I would argue, by a mistaken preconception that he writes as a dogmatic teacher. While it is true that one's predilection toward Christianity affects a predisposition to be sympathetic to Paul, his letters can still appeal to non-Christians, just as Augustine's *Confessions*, a highly religious text, stands as a classic of Western literature, read by the religious and the nonreligious alike. It is much harder to shuck off the sense of pious dogmatism that surrounds Paul than it is for Augustine, but Paul's letters reward the efforts. He remains a powerful writer of forceful rhetoric, and one need not be on his side to listen to him. Just ask the Galatians.

# Chapter 5
# Revelation

## Ancient texts, Revelation, and fantasy Literature

In the earliest written texts, there was war between the gods. The *Enuma Elish*, a Babylonian creation myth from ancient Mesopotamia, describes in vivid detail how one heroic divine figure, Marduk, fought a goddess, Tiamat, who is considered evil by her enemies. In the aftermath of Tiamat's defeat, Marduk slices her in two lengthwise and creates the earth and sky from her filleted body. The death of Tiamat inaugurated the creation of the city-state of Babylon, whose citizens owe their civilization to the triumph of Marduk. The *Enuma Elish* begins a rich literary history of epics such as the *Iliad* and the *Aeneid* in which great wars lead to great civilizations. In almost all epics, two groups vie for supremacy. The epic narrator, with varying degrees of subtlety, sympathizes with one faction and structures the work so that the outcome seems preordained. Civilization itself hangs in the balance. Furthermore, in these battle epics, dualism dominates. That is, almost every character within the work must choose one of two sides; neutrality is rarely allowed. The lasting popularity of works such as these shows that throughout human history, elaborately drawn clashes between good and evil (on the narrator's terms) have enthralled audiences, allowing them to participate vicariously in fictive battles.

In modern times, fantasy literature and movies present a pop culture analogy to epic literature. The draw of fantasy worlds where good and evil collide is exemplified by the enormous popularity of phenomena such as *Star Wars, The Lord of the Rings,* and the Harry Potter books. In spite of the divergent settings of these series, the elements of all three creations have striking commonalities. The characters in these sagas find themselves in the midst of a world disturbed by the emergence of an overwhelming evil power (Darth Vader, Sauron, and Voldemort). All sentient creatures must ally themselves with either the force of evil or the counterforces of good. Those who oppose evil seem drastically inadequate to the task. Their numbers are few, fate seems to work against them, and the powers they wield pale in significance compared to those of the dark side. Even the most potent forces for good (Obi-Wan Kenobi, Gandalf, and Dumbledore) suffer defeat and death when they try to oppose the sway of oppressive evil.

In spite of the long odds, however, hope for evil's ultimate defeat dwells in one seemingly insignificant person (Luke Skywalker, Frodo, and Harry). For reasons that are never explained fully, fate or divine favor or dumb luck has endowed this solitary individual with enough clout and fortitude to face insurmountable odds and destroy the enemy. The readers and viewers know (due to the conventions of the genre) that what seems insurmountable will prove not to be, and in spite of the tension felt in the pages and on the screen, audiences know that in the end, all will be well, and a new, peaceful world will germinate from the seeds of war. In this simple sense, fantasy works update the perennial story begun with the ancient Babylonians. Chaos threatens to overwhelm the earth and human history, but the underlying forces of order rise up when it becomes necessary for them to reassert themselves.

The last book of the New Testament, Revelation, fits somewhere between the *Enuma Elish* and modern fantasy literature. Like the Babylonian epic, it tells a story of divine powers—God and

Satan—that battle for control. In Revelation, what's at stake is whether Earth and its inhabitants will fall under the influence of the good God or the evil Satan. As the *Enuma Elish* ends in the creation of Babylon, so Revelation will end with the creation of the New Heaven and New Earth. Instead of being cut up like Tiamat to form heaven and earth, however, Satan is banished forever into the Lake of Fire. In both cases, though, the supernatural force for order vanquishes the power that chaotically threatens humans, resulting in a well-established peace.

Linguistically, Revelation aims not for the sophistication of epic poetry but rather for vernacular sensibilities. Revelation should be considered popular literature. It too has a fairly simplistic understanding of the forces at play in the world. The entire document unfolds a vision that its author John (*not* the same person who wrote the Gospel of John) received while on the island of Patmos in the Aegean Sea. In his setting—late in the first century on the eastern edge of the Roman Empire—John diagnoses the situation as one in which Satan has control of the power structure of the Roman government, and God's people (the good guys, so to speak) have been marginalized. Revelation is not a sophisticated sociological analysis; it is too blunt for that. It does not encourage contemplation but rather provides a vicarious thrill in seeing how satanic forces and godly ones will eventually clash with one another.

*Star Wars*, *Lord of the Rings*, and the Harry Potter books, therefore, give the modern reader insight into how Revelation might have functioned in its own time. Tolkien's trilogy is particularly illustrative. In 1999 the Modern Library commissioned critics to determine the one hundred greatest novels of the twentieth century. *The Lord of the Rings* did not make the list, but in 2005, when *Time* magazine asked its readers to choose the greatest novels of all time, Tolkien's work garnered the top spot. In spite of Tolkien's eminent work as a literary critic, his fiction is rarely taken seriously as literature. His world of Middle Earth straightforwardly divides into good and bad, conflicts are obviously spelled out for the reader, and nuance does not exist. The same is true for *Star Wars* and Harry Potter. In all these cases, the artist attempts to provide the audience with a rollicking tale. This is not to say that they aren't crafted well but that the craft is meant to have a broad appeal, one that is easily and readily grasped by the vast majority of humans.

Revelation, while having a very serious ethical and hortatory impulse, also engages the imagination. Anachronistically, one could say that Revelation seems very cinematic. It is filled with visual imagery of monsters, disasters, and roiling battles, and the action moves at a rapid pace. In fact, the basic narrative of fantasy literature derives from Revelation. In power—seemingly— is Satan, who can bend society to his will because of his ties to the emperors of Rome. Ordinary citizens must either side with this evil empire or choose loyalty to God. If they do not succumb to the empire, they will undoubtedly, as John implies, undergo hardship, torture, and possibly death. Although the situation seems bleak, all is not lost. The downfall of evil will come at the hands of an unlikely hero—Jesus, who has ignominiously died due to the actions of Rome itself. But like Gandalf (or vice versa), he rises again, much more powerful than he was while alive on the earth. Because Satan and his army have underestimated the might of this single creature, they will be utterly trounced in a final battle, and a new world will arise to supersede the tainted one left behind by Satan.

Two major differences between Revelation and fantasy literature should be noted. First, while using fictional elements and imaginative rhetoric, the author of Revelation clearly assumes that the main characters in his book truly exist. While entertaining, this book does not exist for the sake of entertainment. We might say that it literally wants to scare the hell out of you. Because of its deadly serious exhortative elements, Revelation does not quite conform to modern notions of fiction writing. Most emphatically, the author strongly implies that the final triumph of good over evil at the end of time corresponds to an actual event. John blends together history and imagination so that his work falls somewhere between fiction and nonfiction.

Secondly, the book focuses on both this world and the heaven world, both the world of the present and the afterworld of the future. The material world, the center of things in *Star Wars* and Harry Potter, matters very little to Revelation. What counts is the unseen world and the heavenly existence that will come into being when this world ends. When readers vicariously place themselves into the narrative, they also, in the scheme of the book, determine their fate. Unlike a modern reader of Harry Potter, who can only imaginatively inhabit Hogwarts, readers of Revelation are directed to view the dualistic elements of this vision as absolutely corresponding to the way things are and will be.

## Genre

The last book of the New Testament is commonly known by one of two titles: Revelation or The Apocalypse. Until the fourteenth century, it was known as The Apocalypse, but by the time of the King James translation in 1610, the name Revelation had stuck. Although the etymologies of these two titles are almost exactly the same, the two words convey quite different meanings in modern English. The Greek word *apokalupsis*, from which the English apocalyptic and apocalypticism derive, means the uncovering of something that is hidden. In other parts of the New Testament, especially in Paul's letters, it is usually translated as "revelation." That word means essentially the same as *apokalupsis*, though it often carries religious overtones. In modern usage, however, "apocalypse" conjures up images of the annihilation of the earth or some other cataclysmic event. "Revelation" remains a much more gentle word, generally meaning something like an epiphany, an experience of apprehending new knowledge of some sort.

These two trajectories of this single title—Revelation/ Apocalypse—comprise a fortuitous turn of language, since this document both announces the cataclysmic end of the world and concurrently reveals God's identity and plan to human beings. The odd fact that two etymologically similar words now adhere to two completely different meanings corresponds to the interpretation of the book of Revelation. It both gives one a new perspective and similarly presents images of horror and destruction. The revelation that is uncovered to the author John provokes either terror or comfort or, occasionally, both.

Although it seems bizarre in comparison to the gospels and letters, Revelation fits comfortably into a genre of literature—what we now called apocalyptic literature in honor of this book—common to Judaism and Christianity in the Greco-Roman world. Some stock elements of apocalyptic literature include visionary experience, angels and demons, allegorical beasts and creatures, and heavenly journeys. In apocalyptic works, the action takes place in both heavenly and earthly planes, with the narrator inhabiting both worlds. Usually the narrative includes large sections of foreshadowing in which the visionary speaker receives instruction from divine forces about what will take place in the future. All of these formal elements appear in Revelation. Just as contemporary readers know they are encountering a fairy tale when they hear the words "once upon a time" or when the story is about princesses, knights, and goblins, John's audience would have immediately put this particular work into the expectations that come with reading particular genres.

Apocalyptic literature was characterized not only by formal elements but also by theological contemplation. Almost every apocalypse stems from an experience of feeling overwhelmed by chaotic, oppressive forces of persecution or evil. Jewish apocalypses prior to Revelation often arose from either actual pogroms or from powers that were intent on destroying elements of Judaism. In response to what they see as the victimization of

God's people at the hands of sinners, apocalyptic authors bluntly ask why God allows such ill-treatment. As one Jewish writing contemporary to Revelation asks, "For if you destroy your city and deliver up your country to those who hate us, how will the name of Israel be remembered again?" (2 Bar. 3:5). God answers this question and countless others like it by saying that God has not forgotten, and that evil will be vanquished in the future. Apocalyptic writings, sometimes softly and often vehemently, accuse God of willful indifference to suffering. But they all then forcefully counter their rhetorical accusations with proclamations of God's ultimate victory.

Revelation, which dates to the end of the first century, addresses itself to Christians who feel dominated by the Roman Empire and its culture. In one of John's visions, he sees the "souls of those who had been slaughtered for the word of God," and they wonder whether God has forgotten them: "How long will it be before you judge and avenge our blood on the inhabitants of the earth?" They are told to wait just a bit longer but assured that vengeance is coming (6:9–11). This explicit cry of anguish, coupled with the typical situation of apocalyptic, indicates that John's audience was troubled. They were churches on the western edge of ancient Asia (present-day Turkey), who felt threatened by the imperial forces. To assuage their anxieties, John addresses them with exhortatory letters (chaps. 2–3) and with his apocalyptic vision, urging them not to give up hope. The most common refrain in these letters is a reward to "one who conquers," indicating that the Asian churches are involved in a metaphorical war. The explicit command in the letters not to acquiesce to the enemy corresponds to the vision, as the warning to the churches is backed up with story of what will happen to them if they do not. They should not capitulate because God will destroy his/their enemy soon. They will be better off if God finds them on the winning side.

The genre of apocalyptic, therefore, lies somewhere between allegory and myth. It is allegorical in the sense that many of its symbols correspond directly to specific entities. To cite the most obvious example, in chapter 17, John describes a woman who is clothed in purple and scarlet and is "drunk with the blood of the saints." The name "Babylon the Great" is tattooed on her forehead, and she sits on seven mountains. John says that her name is a "mystery," but it does not take much cleverness to solve it. She is clearly Rome, and almost anyone living in the empire would have recognized her as such, due to the famous seven hills of Rome. It would be like an American apocalypticist writing, "On her head was 'the big D,' and she sat on the plain in the land of the lone star." It may not be immediately obvious, but with a little thought, anyone who knew basic American geography would know the author spoke of Dallas, Texas.

Yet most of the symbols in Revelation have a broad range of meanings, and the narrative as a whole goes well beyond the confines of first century Asia Minor. This mythic quality has captivated readers who might be oblivious to the allegorical elements. History's imagination has found a veritable mine of material in Revelation, demonstrating its power as myth. It has proven remarkably malleable in the hands of songwriters, painters, sculptors, soothsayers, screenwriters, poets, charlatans, and street-preachers. The stark battle between evil and good seems to continually find an audience eager to understand their own world through the lens of this Christian apocalyptic.

## The characterization of Jesus

Because Revelation's plot depends largely upon action, it does not spend much time on character development. Yet the opening words of the book, "the revelation of Jesus Christ," proclaim that the entirety of the vision centers on Jesus himself. These words contain a grammatical ambiguity. The "of" could function like the phrase "loaf of bread," in which both words name the same object. If read this way, Jesus Christ will be revealed; he himself is the revelation. The "of" could also denote possession, indicating that the revelation belongs to Jesus and has its source in him, as in the phrase "wrath of God." This ambiguity need not be decided as either/or. Clearly the book contains a special message from Christ, but at the same time, the book carefully reveals the identity of the messenger. What will be revealed in this book belongs to Jesus alone, and the content of the prophecy (1:3) will explain who he is.

John, like Paul, has almost no interest at all in Jesus' earthly existence. In keeping with the conventions of apocalyptic, he portrays Jesus through a series of images, not through a continuous story. Perhaps the boldest feature of Revelation is the way that John combines different strains of traditional understandings of Jesus. He appears prominently in four scenes: the opening vision in 1:12–20, the throne room of God in 5:1–14, the final battle in 19:11–21, and the closing dialogue in 22. In each of these passages, John portrays Jesus in strikingly different ways. The amalgamation of these portrayals gives Revelation its distinctive understanding of Jesus.

The first time Jesus appears, he overwhelms the senses:

> I [John] turned to see whose voice it was that spoke to me, and on
> turning I saw seven golden lampstands, and in the midst of the
> lampstands I saw one like the Son of Man, clothed with a long robe
> and with a golden sash across his chest. His head and his hair
> were white as white wool, white as snow; his eyes were like a flame of
> fire, his feet were like burnished bronze, refined as in a furnace,
> and his voice was like the sound of many waters. In his right hand
> he held seven stars, and from his mouth came a sharp, two-edged
> sword, and his face was like the sun shining with full force. (1:12–16)

Each element of this vision contains symbolic importance. The whiteness of the hair and head conveys purity, the sword coming out of the mouth demonstrates the power of his words, and the blazing eyes illustrate his piercing insight. On a literal level this first presentation of Jesus as the "Son of Man" is grotesque enough for John to fall down "as if dead." The brightness of the face, hair, eyes, and sash, combined with a voice that sounds like thunderous waters, presents Jesus as a completely otherworldly persona. He is both real and a phantasm, a once-human person that has now transcended earthly existence.

The second scene (chap. 5) references Jesus' crucifixion through the allegorical figure of a lamb. As John stands at the throne of God, in the midst of heavenly creatures that are worshiping, God produces a scroll. An angel asks, "Who is worthy to open the scroll and break its seals?" (5:2), but no one comes forward. As John laments the fact that no one can open it, one of the elders says to him, "Do not weep. See, the Lion of the tribe of Judah, the Root of David, has conquered, so that he can open the scroll and its seven seals" (5:5). Just then, Jesus makes his appearance: "Then I saw ... a Lamb standing as if it had been slaughtered, having seven horns and seven eyes, which are the seven spirits of God sent out into all the earth" (5:6). The elders praise his ability to open the scroll as they sing to him, "You are worthy to take the scroll and to open its seals, for you were slaughtered" (5:9). If the first portrayal of Jesus was overwhelming in its majesty, this vision overwhelms because of its gruesomeness. It is both pitiful and monstrous. Slaughtering a lamb would involve slitting its throat, so this creature would seem to have a gaping wound in its neck, along with seven horns and seven eyes, scattered, one supposes, throughout the rest of its body. John says that he is "standing," as if to counter a false supposition that the lamb has actually died. Although the elders had described him as a lion, this repellent image runs exactly opposite to his introduction expected. It looks more like prey than predator. The strange combination of the name "Lion of the Tribe of Judah" attached to a slaughtered lamb creates a paradoxical Jesus—one who conquers and who has been momentarily conquered by death.

Except for a brief mention of a threatened infant in 12:5, Jesus appears for a third time toward the end of the book, in the climactic battle between heavenly forces for good and earthly forces of evil:

Then I saw heaven opened, and there was a white horse! Its rider is called Faithful and True, and in righteousness he judges and makes war. His eyes are like a flame of fire, and on his head are many diadems; and he has a name inscribed that no one knows but himself. He is clothed in a robe dipped in blood, and his name is called The Word of God. And the armies of heaven, wearing fine linen, white and pure, were following him on white horses. From his mouth comes a sharp sword with which to strike down the nations, and he will rule them with a rod of iron; he will tread the wine press of the fury of the wrath of God the Almighty. On his robe and on his thigh he has a name inscribed, "King of kings and Lord of lords. (19:11–16)

The white robe and the blazing eyes identify this person as the "one like the Son of Man" in chapter 1, and the blood on his robe recalls the slaughtered lamb of chapter 5. This time Jesus appears on Earth instead of heaven, and he shows up in order to demonstrate concretely the latent power indicated in the heavenly throne room. Unlike either of those previous manifestations, this image of Jesus presents a dynamic figure who is almost human. He has not lost all his grotesqueness—he strikes down the enemy with the sword protruding from his mouth—but he seems not very different from a valiant field marshal.

Jesus' fourth and final appearance shifts away from visual imagery and relics instead on auditory experience. After the final battle with evil, God and Jesus make their home on a refurbished Earth: "See, the home of God is among mortals. He will dwell with them as their God; they will be his peoples, and God himself will be with them" (21:3). After this, divine voices address John twice more:

And the one who was seated on the throne said, "See, I am making all things new." Also he said, "Write this, for these words are trustworthy and true." Then he said to me, "It is done! I am the Alpha and the Omega, the beginning and the end. To the thirsty

I will give water as a gift from the spring of the water of life. Those who conquer will inherit these things, and I will be their God and they will be my children. (21:5–7)

"See, I am coming soon; my reward is with me, to repay according to everyone's work. I am the Alpha and the Omega, the first and the last, the beginning and the end." (22:12–13)

Determining the speaker of these sentences proves difficult. Both verses recall chapter 1, where God uses the same title, " 'I am the Alpha and the Omega,' says the Lord God, who is and who was and who is to come" (1:8). In 22:12, however, Jesus must surely be the speaker who talks of coming soon. Throughout this final chapter, John links together a series of quotations in a manner that masks the identity of who is speaking. An angel addresses John in verse 9, but by verse 12, the speaker has surely changed. In verses 14–15, one cannot tell whether the speaker is John or the angel or Jesus or God, but Jesus himself breaks in at verse 16 to say "It is I, Jesus."

In closing out his vision, John presents the implications of Jesus as "Word of God" in a very literal sense. Jesus the material being dissolves into speech. In fact, all pictorial representations of divinity tend to fall away in the new heaven and new earth. Although the throne of the Lamb occupies a central location in this paradise, the Lamb itself does not appear. It seems that the title of Word of God that was given to Jesus-the-general was foreshadowing his status at the end of time. After the battle on earth, when God speaks, the voice says, "It is I, Jesus." The words of God and the Word of God unite into a synthesis that makes it almost impossible to distinguish one from another. The previous incarnations of Jesus have been leading up to a nonvisual, nonmaterial unification with God.

For the writer of Revelation, therefore, the resurrection of Jesus signifies a transfiguration that utterly transforms the man who lived on earth, gathered disciples, and was crucified. The implication of "making all things new" applies to Jesus as well. That human figure serves only as a precursor to the heavenly figure that John encounters as a divine statue, a disfigured lamb, a superhuman general, and a disembodied voice. By combining these images John wrenches Jesus from the earthly figure that serves as the central character of the gospels. He returns Jesus to God, finally blending the two together into a seamless unit.

## Ideology and structure

If maddening in its details, the broad structure of Revelation proves relatively straightforward. The book begins with an introduction in chapter 1, where John presents his reasons for writing and the first vision of Jesus. Then, in chapters 2 and 3, he writes seven letters to churches in Asia Minor, in which he urges them to hold fast to Christian teaching. The main section of Revelation begins in chapter 4 and continues through chapter 20. Here John presents a whirlwind of imagery and action, oscillating between action on earth and encounters in heaven. There is a break between chapters 11 and 12, when the primary locale shifts from heaven (chaps. 1–11) to Earth (chaps. 12–20). All the action of Revelation leads toward the climax of chapters 19 and 20, when Jesus, on horseback, takes charge of the heavenly army, defeats Satan and his troops, culminating the battle by throwing Satan and his followers into a lake of fire. The denouement of 21–22 presents what John calls a "new heaven and a new earth," a place that God's followers will enjoy an eternal peace.

Revelation strongly adheres to a dualistic scheme, best exemplified by the letter John writes to the church in Laodicea:

> I know your works; you are neither cold nor hot. I wish that
> you were either cold or hot. So because you are lukewarm,
> and neither hot nor cold, I am about to spit you out of my mouth.
> (3:15–16)

John, like most apocalyptic writers, has no use for moderation. He does not, like Aristotle or Buddha, propose a middle way as the safest and most reasonable path. Every single character—beast, human, divine or demonic being—in Revelation functions either as a paragon of godliness or an embodiment of pure evil. The only exceptions would be the four horsemen who spring into life as the Lamb breaks open the scroll. They themselves have no personality, but they do act as instruments of God's wrath upon the wholly wicked inhabitants of the earth. Other beings that populate John's vision neatly divide into two camps. Allies of God include: angels (1:8, 12:7, 22:8), two witnesses (11:3), 144,000 male virgins (14:1–4), a woman who gives birth to a son (12:1), John and Jesus. On the other side of the divide are: Satan, the dragon (12), a beast from the sea (13:1), a beast from the land (13:11), and the Whore of Babylon (17). When a reader is given the choice to side with beasts and dragons or angels and elders, there is clearly not much subtle characterization going on.

Revelation's dualism recalls the ironic joke: "There are two kinds of people in the world: those that divide the world into two kinds of people in the world and those that don't." John clearly does divide the world into two types. This division seems clearest in chapters 13–14, in which two beasts arise, one from the sea and one from the land. (These monstrous figures hearken back to Leviathan and Behemoth, the land and sea monsters that play a prominent role in Job.) The first beast "was allowed to make war on the saints and to conquer them" (13:7). The second speaks on behalf of the first and "makes the earth and its inhabitants worship the first beast" (13:12). No one can engage in commerce without paying obeisance to the beasts and demonstrating their loyalty with the mark of the beast—the number 666. Both of the beasts show homage to the dragon, whom the text explicitly identifies as Satan (12:9).

John then presents the readers with a choice:

Those who worship the beast and its image, and receive a mark on their foreheads or on their hands, they will also drink the wine of God's wrath, poured unmixed into the cup of his anger, and they will be tormented with fire and sulfur in the presence of the holy angels and in the presence of the Lamb. And the smoke of their torment goes up forever and ever. There is no rest day or night for those who worship the beast and its image and for anyone who receives the mark of its name.

Here is a call for the endurance of the saints, those who keep the commandments of God and hold fast to the faith of Jesus. (14:9–12)

Simply put, the author says, "Eternal punishment or eternal peace, the choice is yours." The entirety of the ethics of Revelation is summed up in this last verse. Although he says that the readers should "keep the commandments," he only briefly mentions any particular actions the readers should take. The second part of the verse takes precedence. Holding fast to the faith of Jesus is the singular injunction of this book. Do this, he says, and your safety is assured.

The dualism of Revelation has tended to create a dual reaction. No other book of the New Testament has provoked such a sharp distinction between popular and scholarly reception. It has often been eagerly read and applauded in grassroots movements, particularly among those on the margins of society. Such groups as Jehovah's Witnesses and the Seventh Day Adventists take Revelation as their primary impetus for breaking away from other forms of Christianity. The recent success in the United States of the *Left Behind* series, a fictionalized version of the end of the world based loosely on Revelation, also points to its popular appeal (70 million books sold). Great scholarly interpreters of the Bible, however, often seem embarrassed by Revelation. The two most influential figures of the Reformation—John Calvin and Martin Luther—had grave doubts about Revelation's value. Calvin wrote a commentary on every book of the Bible except that one, and Luther wrote that Revelation was "neither apostolic nor prophetic."

D. H. Lawrence, the English novelist and poet, was particularly appalled by the dualism of this work. Toward the end of his life, he scathingly attacked Revelation because of its ideology. He finds the book utterly distasteful and inartistic:

> In Jesus' day, the inwardly strong men everywhere had lost their desire to rule on earth. They wished to withdraw their strength from earthly rule and earthly power, and to apply it to another form of life. Then the weak began to rouse up and to feel *inordinately* conceited; they began to express their rampant hate of the "obvious" strong ones, the men in worldly power.
>
> So that religion, the Christian religion especially, became dual. The religion of the strong taught renunciation and love. And the religion of the weak taught *down with the strong and the powerful, and let the poor be glorified* ...
>
> The grand biblical authority for this cry is the Apocalypse.[1]

More succinctly, Lawrence draws a parallel between Revelation and Eden, when he says, "There crept into the New Testament the grand Christian enemy, the Power-spirit. At the very last moment, when the devil had been so beautifully shut out, in he slipped, dressed in Apocalyptic disguise, and enthroned himself at the end of the book as Revelation."[2] What rankles Lawrence is the book's push toward a mass collective sense of humanity that will inherit the world at the expense of the powerful ruling elite. He finds in Revelation too great a sense of *schadenfreude*—the glee that envious people feel when their enemies get what's coming to them.

For Lawrence, the last book of the New Testament unravels the grand vision of the gospels. There Jesus displayed brave individuality and a universal love that transcended societal norms. He was concerned not with gaining power but with losing it. Lawrence rightly sees that Revelation appeals to those powerless masses that find themselves on the outer edges of the circle of power. He, along with many others, see Revelation not only as distasteful but inherently dangerous. John's vision lends itself to a desire for vindication, especially among groups that Lawrence sneeringly calls "the weak."

On the other hand, one of the best-known English musical works revels in the triumphalism that Lawrence detests. George Frederic Handel's "Hallelujah" chorus from *Messiah* comes directly from verses in Revelation:

> Hallelujah! For the Lord God omnipotent reigneth (19:6, KJV)
>
> The kingdoms of this world are become the kingdoms of our Lord, and of his Christ; and he shall reign for ever and ever. (11:15, KJV)
>
> And he hath on his vesture and on his thigh a name written, KING OF KINGS, AND LORD OF LORDS. (19:16, KJV)

The three verses comprising the lyrics are tied together by the word "reign" in the first two lines. The staccato rhythms of Handel's music, the bright trumpet score, and the lyrics of Revelation, when combined together, exude majesty and triumph. Within the sequence of *Messiah*, Handel places this chorus at a pivotal position, to express the ultimate triumph of life over death by means of the resurrection of Jesus. The words from Revelation, the coda of the New Testament, serve his purpose of expressing ultimate victory in song.

The context of these verses gives an added dimension to the force of Handel's work. The main refrain comes from the end of Revelation, just before the climactic battle between the forces of God and Jesus and the forces of Satan. The author John hears a chorus of voices in heaven, certain of the outcome of the impending battle (presented here in verse form):

> After this I heard what seemed to be the loud voice of a great multitude in
> Heaven, saying,

"Hallelujah!
Salvation and glory and power to our God,
For his judgments are true and just;
he has judged the great whore
who corrupted the earth with her fornication,
and he has avenged on her the blood of his servants."
Once more they said,
"Hallelujah!
The smoke goes up from her forever and ever."
And the twenty-four elders and the four living creatures fell
   down and
worshiped God who is seated on the throne, saying,
"Amen. Hallelujah!"
And from the throne came a voice saying,
"Praise our God,
all you his servants,
and all who fear him,
small and great."
Then I heard what seemed to be the voice of a great multitude,
   like the
sound of many waters and like the sound of mighty thunderpeals,
   crying out,
"Hallelujah!
For the Lord our God
the Almighty reigns. (19:1–6)

This song, ending in Handel's line, highlights both the victory
and destruction that run as parallel themes in Revelation. God's
reign endures and the Whore of Babylon is destroyed. The two
are inseparable from one another. Handel's quotation of God
reigning "forever and ever" finds its echo in the ruins of the
allegorical city/woman Babylon: "The smoke goes up from her
forever and ever." (19:3)

Revelation is a war story and a fantasy story. The belligerence of
the narrative involves lots of killing of those the author considers

evil. The fantasy element, however, encourages the reader not to dwell on the dead long enough to sympathize with them. This book, like many Westerns and action films, glories in violent deaths...but only of those who truly "deserve" it. (To return to my earlier examples, viewers do not shed tears over the slaughter of Tolkien's orcs or Darth Vader's storm troopers.) On a surface level, such works appeal to a sense of justice against oppression. The author John is certainly not wrong in depicting Roman power as beholden to commerce and inimical to those who do not kowtow to imperial whims. It is this sense of justice that makes Revelation's dualism attractive. Handel gloriously celebrates the transfer of kingship from this world to God in the stirring refrain of the "Hallelujah" chorus. Even those not of a religious bent can be swayed by his celebration of victory.

Where, then, does the opposite reaction—Lawrence's, for example—spring? Just as many critics point out the dangerous desensitizing tendencies of violence in modern cinema (and, often, its accompanying misogyny), if one dwells on the literal aspects of Revelation, one is forced to think about the individual bodies burned up by God. From a critical perspective, Revelation promotes a highly questionable ethical stance, one that praises a collective desire for mass death. The world seldom presents real people and real situations with the lack of nuance that Revelation does. People do encounter good and evil, but contrary to Revelation's structure, they are usually mixed together in varying percentages.

# Chapter 6
# The New Testament, bound

In the previous chapters, we have explored various books of the New Testament as individual writings, or, in the case of Paul, as writings penned by one individual. In this last chapter, we read the New Testament not as discrete independent parts but as a singular collection.

A literary reading of the New Testament in its entirety presents formidable difficulties, given its collective nature. Most pointedly, each writing asserts its independence and resists assimilation with the rest. Some of the books do, of course, display a natural affinity with their neighbors—Paul's letters, Luke-Acts, and the Johannine letters in particular—but even these do not belie evidence that would necessarily welcome anthologizing. No one claims, for instance, that the author of Hebrews envisaged his treatise would forever find itself in front of James's letter. Due to the vagaries of historical circumstances, however, for the last 1600 years people have, in fact, read them in tandem due to their placement within the New Testament.

Collecting the writings into the New Testament inevitably shifts their original meanings. Putting 1 Timothy, which was not written by Paul, alongside authentic Pauline letters inevitably affects the reception of both the authentic and the inauthentic documents. Once all these letters are bound together, the physical reality of the binding itself implies a unity where one did not exist originally and historically. Scholars, usually guided by historical concerns, have therefore been very hesitant to make claims that begin, "The New Testament teaches..." They feel that such statements distort the original intentions of the authors. Scholarship instead aims for the particular, preferring the Johannine, the Lukan, or the Pauline voice, and then comparing and contrasting these voices. For a literary approach also, this seems the most appropriate starting point for exploring a text. To attend properly to the literary features of Mark or Revelation, it would be distortive and misleading to blend in aspects of other New Testament writings. Thus the previous chapters of this introductory text.

Not to address the New Testament as a whole, however, willfully ignores the history of its influence. In contrast to scholarly endeavors, Christian vernacular emphatically does include talk about what "the Bible says" or "the New Testament's teaching." Pragmatically, a literary reading must attend to the entire collection. Otherwise the reader approaches the New Testament with a latent belligerence toward history itself. The vast majority of the New Testament's readers have thought of the writings as forming a unit, so we too, if we are not to live in a utopia, examine how they might work as a single collection.

As an imaginative but realistic starting point, therefore, this last chapter makes an assumption about the entire New Testament that the previous chapters made about each gospel, about Paul's letters, and about Revelation: that the text as it currently exists constitutes a single document. This starting point is imaginative because we know that these writings were not originally conceived as parts of a whole. It is realistic, though, because as history abundantly makes clear, they *can be* read as a whole. It must be noted, however, that a holistic reading does not imply a singularity. Searching for the New Testament's meaning begins with an awareness of the unmistakable plurality of voices within the binding.

# The Development of a Canon

The word Bible derives from the plural Greek noun, *biblia*, which simply means books. When the terminology of "the books" morphed into the Bible, it raised an interesting question. With this title do we mean that it is singular or plural? The historical process by which Christians shifted their focus from the scriptures to one scripture helps address the question.

As Christianity developed from a very small group of Jesus' followers to a religion that eventually populated the entire Mediterranean area, they increasingly relied on written documents. From its earliest origins, the Christian religion valued the concept of "Scripture," mainly because Christianity was an offshoot of Judaism. Every single writer of the New Testament views the Hebrew scriptures as authoritative and normative. It is not surprising that as Christians increased in number, they also widened the boundaries of their scripture to include books beyond those found in the Hebrew Bible. At an early stage, certain Christian writings had garnered a widespread popularity among readers, a popularity that eventually transformed into authority.

In 367, the Bishop of Alexandria, an influential writer named Athanasius, wrote a letter that, in an imitation of Luke's prologue, gives advice about what Christians should read:

> It seemed good to me also, having been urged thereto by true brethren, and having learned from the beginning, to set before you the books included in the canon, and handed down, and accredited as divine.

He then lists the twenty-seven books that comprise the New Testament. His word "canon" originally meant a measuring rod but later came to denote a collection of texts that a particular group finds authoritative. By the time Athanasius wrote, there was widespread (but not universal) agreement that these twenty-seven

The New Testament as Literature

documents were qualitatively different from all other written products. The canonical writings, according to Athanasius, give clear parameters of Christian identity. The decision to mark off a canon essentially says, "If anyone wants to understand Christianity, read these documents. No other words express our worldview and beliefs so perfectly."

The process by which the New Testament was formed began well before Athanasius. Over the three hundred years that separate Paul and Athanasius, the canon grew into its final form by a combination of organic processes and formal decisions. It is important to recognize both the "bottom up" and the "top down" forces that shaped both what was excluded and what was included. By the second century, the gospels and Paul's letters had acquired a substantial influence in many parts of the Mediterranean world. During this period, Christians constituted a small minority of the Roman Empire, and they were not bound by any central authority. No one person or group had the clout to decree absolutely what books were allowed and which were disdained. Yet by the year 200 CE, we have substantial evidence that the four gospels and Paul's letters in particular were held in high regard. One important document from around 170, the Muratorian Fragment, describes the particular books "held sacred in the esteem of the Church." This claim is descriptive, not prescriptive; the document itself is the oldest known list of the books in the New Testament. As Christian leaders made statements on canonical books, they did not dictate their will so much as confirm what was already taking place.

Later on, as Christianity became more powerful and centralized, bishops drew up more explicit criteria—the most important of which was apostolic authorship—that determined what they would include and exclude. Some writings, now known as the New Testament Apocrypha, were explicitly rejected from consideration because they were considered too deviant from those that had already been chosen and from orthodox claims of the church. It is important to recognize that even in these executive decisions, the bishops had some pragmatic aims. To return to my discussion of the function of literature, the leadership of the church put their blessing on texts that had already proved themselves useful. The texts that eventually made it into the New Testament were documents that readers found engaging. Individuals, even those (like bishops) who have power, cannot declaim to the public what counts as literature. Canon always reflects the interests and desires of a particular community of readers, and the formation of the New Testament was driven by a communitarian impulse.

Athanasius, though, relates canonicity to divinity; for him, these books have a divine imprint and provide what he calls "fountains of salvation." His description belongs to the realm of theology, not literary study. Putting the claim to divine origin aside, canonization has far-reaching literary implications. Given that Christians claimed (and still claim) that these and only these writings are inspired, what difference does that make? It is clear that each of the books of the New Testament achieves a different valence when put alongside the other canonical works. Some of these books display a strongly congruent relationship. For instance, in Matthew, 1 Thessalonians, 2 Peter, and Revelation—four otherwise very different types of writing—the second coming of Jesus is likened to a thief coming at night. Other books make uneasy bedfellows. The epistle of 1 Peter, for instance, urges its audience to accept the emperor's authority and to honor him accordingly. The author of Revelation would consider that advice to be utterly deplorable, if not satanic.

Just because these books have been canonized does not mean that their distinctive features disappear. Nor does it mean that contradictions between the books lessen. Taking the canon seriously means that we must look for a model to understand this disparate yet unified collection.

# Analogies, models, and metaphors

The biblical canon has no clear parallel in literature. Consider the discussion of the Western canon that sometimes dominates literature departments. The Western Canon refers to literary works that can rightly be considered classics, texts that helped form Western culture and that deserve ongoing appreciation. Whenever people debate the Western canon, they do so primarily to discuss what should be added or taken away from it. Sometimes the discussion veers into the more basic question of whether the canon itself is desirable, measurable, or necessary. The New Testament canon, on the other hand, has such a long history that it is no longer negotiable. Since the books center upon Jesus and his followers in the first and second centuries, it also represents a thematic and temporal unity that the Western canon does not.

If the literary canon fails as an analogy, another parallel might be the collected works of a single author. Critics often speak of the Shakespearean canon, the collection of all the Bard's plays and poetry. College courses, many of which are simply titled "Shakespeare," implicitly adhere to ideas of a canon. This does not indicate that all the plays need to be read together, but such an option is warranted. Techniques or characterizations in Macbeth might illuminate an encounter with Hamlet. More directly, Henry V clearly extends the story and characterizations begun in Henry IV, parts 1 and 2, and a reading of any single one of these plays benefits from knowledge of the other two. The word *Shakespearean* would have no discernable meaning apart from collecting substantial chunks of his work into a larger framework.

Construing the New Testament as an analogy to the collected works of Shakespeare brings theology to the fore. This analogy has force primarily for those who discern an authorial voice that grounds all the documents. Certainly some Christians view God as the ultimate author of the Bible who speaks through the putative human authors. Without positing this ultimate authority, however, the analogy tends to weaken.

Since the New Testament lacks any clear canonical parallels, it is useful to think of it in relationship to other aesthetic experiences. Suppose that a reader approached the New Testament as a book and read it in canonical order, from Matthew to Revelation. Although it starts like a single novel with Matthew's narrative, it quickly shifts to other points of view once the reader gets to Mark, Luke, John, and Acts. Then, with Paul's letters, the New Testament leaves narrative altogether and becomes ethical and exhortative. All the letters between Acts and Revelation confront the reader with propositional rhetoric. These letters do not explicitly recall the events of the gospels and Acts, but a reader can certainly make connections between the letters' language about Jesus and the gospels' presentations of him. Revelation returns to narrative and closes out the book in dramatic fashion.

As this hypothetical reader makes her way through the New Testament, she will be governed by the temporality of the experience itself. By attending to the elements of plot, character development, and linguistic clues, the reader attends to the rhythms of the language. Of course, the reader will also make connections between the early content of the text and whatever her eyes happen to be scanning at the moment. In this first reading, however, the connections can only go backward. That is, when a reader finds herself at 1 Timothy, she cannot yet consider Revelation. Only after the entire New Testament is read can the reader mull over the entirety. On a second reading, the experience will be quite different. Then the reader can think backward and forward, knowing the contents of the whole.

These two modes of reading suggest two models for thinking about the New Testament canon. A first reading might be similar to hearing a piece of music. Just as a listener cannot literally hear the entire piece at once, so the first time reader's experience is governed by the temporal nature of reading. Once the reader finishes the last chapter, however, the model of visual art seems more appropriate than that of music. Upon completing the New Testament, a reader does not need to view the books sequentially but rather spatially. She can see it like a complex painting, shifting her focus to various elements upon the canvas while also attending to how these elements work together.

Of these two models, the visual one applies to more readers. Readers occasionally do start with Matthew and read straight through to Revelation, but this is rare. Given a choice between a painting and a sonata as a model, most New Testament readers would opt for the former, primarily because of the abrupt shifts in tone and narrative voice. The various books blend into one another not in a linear or temporal way but in a conceptual framework. Readers of the New Testament often jump from one story to another. A reading of the temptation of Jesus in Mark likely would be augmented by the similar story in either Matthew or Luke, where Satan appears. This story brings to mind the nature of temptation in James, who says "when desire has conceived, it gives birth to sin, and that sin, when it is fully grown, gives birth to death" (1:15). Or the gospel account might lead the reader to turn to Hebrews where the author highlights Jesus' sinlessness or to Revelation, where Satan appears quite prominently. Canon provides many opportunities for meandering, for allowing one's gaze to roam in many directions.

A visual metaphor that works very well for conceptualizing the New Testament is a photographic mosaic. In the last twenty years, sophisticated computer programs have spawned this new type of pop art. Like traditional tile mosaics, a photographic mosaic is comprised of smaller pieces. In photographic mosaics, however, the smaller images are photographs rather than solidly colored pieces. A person can load hundreds or thousands of photographs into a software library from which images will be drawn. Then the

1. Jesus Icon (composed of paintings of Jesus)

user will input a photograph or painting to serve as a composite image. The program will then arrange the individual photographs as a series of rectangles on a grid (see illustration). Close up, each photo retains its integrity, but at a distance, the composite comes into view. A user can even make each piece of the photographic mosaic a variation of the large image. For instance, loading hundreds of photographs of roses into a library can then generate a large single rose made from the pixellated smaller roses.

To read the New Testament as a single document means viewing it as something like a photographic mosaic. The various books of the New Testament function as the tiles. Each of these clearly stands alone as an interpretive portrait of Jesus. As separate pieces, these portraits can be widely divergent, and with a close-up view, it is almost impossible to see them as compatible. From a broad view—the view demanded by a mosaic—a distinguishable if fuzzy portrait starts to come into view. From far away, the individual character of the tiles gives way to a generalized portrait.

In what follows, I sketch out a brief discussion of the New Testament with the metaphor of a photographic mosaic in mind. This entails thinking about various books of the New Testament as particular interpretations of Jesus that contribute to a larger interpretation. Yet I do not leave behind the musical metaphor completely. To take the canon as it stands also means giving the gospels temporal prominence and thinking of the rest of the writers as commenting upon the previous stories.

## The problems and possibilities of the four-fold gospel

At an early stage in Christian history, around the year 180 CE, a writer named Irenaeus argued that it was natural and necessary to have four gospels. In an argument that sounds extraordinarily strained to modern ears, he writes:

> It is not possible that the Gospels can be either more or fewer in number than they are. For, since there are four zones of the world in which we live, and four principal winds, while the Church is scattered throughout all the world, and the pillar and ground of the Church is the Gospel and the spirit of life; it is fitting that she should have four pillars.

His writing is the earliest concrete evidence for the authoritative status of the gospels that eventually made it into the Christian Bible. Although many other gospels, written in an astonishingly wide variety of genres and containing divergent subject matter, were known to Irenaeus, the universe itself demanded that only these four could form "pillars" of Christian faith. In a later section, he castigates the practice of certain Christian communities that latch on to only one gospel. For Irenaeus, the cosmos itself ordains that Matthew, Mark, Luke, and John belong together. To take his metaphor quite seriously means that reading even three of the gospels without the fourth would shake the foundations of church doctrine.

There is no way to discern if Irenaeus's mystical argument found widespread agreement, but soon afterward, almost all Christians were claiming that their understanding of Jesus depended upon four separate but complementary stories. They present an opportunity to explore singularity with plurality because together they are the plural gospels that impart the one gospel. With four stories come four Jesuses, or four interpretations of Jesus. Sometimes these gospel accounts seem benignly complementary, but often they are jarringly contradictory.

This contradiction shows up especially clearly when putting John alongside any of the Synoptics. Specifically, the two traditions conflict most with regard to the passion stories. In Mark, on the night before his crucifixion, Jesus conveys the dread of his imminent death with some of his most famous words:

> They went to a place called Gethsemane; and he said to his disciples, "Sit here while I pray." He took with him Peter and James and John, and began to be distressed and agitated. And said to them, "I am deeply grieved, even to death; remain here, and keep awake." And going a little farther, he threw himself on the ground and prayed that, if it were possible, the hour might pass from him. He said,

"Abba, Father, for you all things are possible; remove this cup from me; yet, not what I want, but what you want." (14:32–36)

Although Jesus has foretold his death three times in Mark, he faces heartrending turmoil when the moment actually arrives. In his hour of greatest emotional agony, his disciples fail him again (they fall asleep instead of keeping watch), increasing his isolation. In the prayer itself, he addresses God with the words a child would use when pleading with a parent. He has no one to turn to, except for God, and he apparently knows God will likely turn a deaf ear to his request. The pathos of Jesus' situation seems as obvious here as at any episode in the gospels. Shortly afterward, his agony reaches its peak when his emotional distress is coupled with the physical suffering of crucifixion. Then he realizes the full force of God's remoteness and cries, "My God, my God, why have you forsaken me?" (15:34).

In contrast to Mark's portrayal, John's Jesus seems strikingly stoic with regard to his death. In fact, John's Jesus seems to peer into Mark's garden scene only to mock Jesus' prayer. In John, just before he enters Jerusalem for the last time, Jesus says, "Now my soul is troubled; and what shall I say—'Father, save me from this hour'? No, it is for this reason I have come to this hour. Father, glorify your name" (12:27–28). He ponders the possibility that he might ask for God's deliverance, as Mark's Jesus did, but scoffs at that option. This Jesus knows with certainty that his death will occur soon, but he controls his own destiny. Earlier, in a discourse where he compares himself to a shepherd, he avows his control with boldness: "For this reason the Father loves me, because I lay down my life in order to take it up again. No one takes it from me, but I lay it down of my own accord. I have power to lay it down, and I have power to take it up again." (10:17–18). On the cross, he speaks robotically and without emotion: "I thirst." "Woman, behold your son." "Son, behold your mother." "It is finished." He displays remarkable control throughout John's passion narrative ("passion," which means suffering, is actually a misnomer for John's gospel) by instructing the soldiers to arrest him, carrying his own cross, and debating with Pilate.

Reading these two gospels together presents a series of dilemmas. Could both of these be true? Is one more historical and the other fanciful? Does John's account try to correct what he sees as an embarrassingly weak Jesus in Mark? To read the gospels together means coming to grips with contradiction. One way to deal with it is to harmonize the two accounts. That is, assert that Jesus did *truly* suffer in John and that he covers it up or, conversely, that he does not *truly* agonize in Mark. He prays to God with only a minimal amount of pleading, and that is his slight nod to a natural human impulse. Both of these harmonizations clearly violate the narratives by not taking either seriously. Another option, one taken by historians, is to claim that Mark's Jesus stands close to the historical circumstances, with an emphasis upon Jesus' humanity and that John's Jesus has no historical basis. John has theologized Jesus, making him divine rather than human. This reading only works by giving priority to Mark and subjugating John. Both options distort the text by imposing nontextual criteria on the gospels. How then can both of these be read together without making one subservient to the other?

If we think of the gospels as portraits, the problem of inconsistency dissolves. If an art gallery includes a series of portraits of a famous figure—George Washington, for example— it would be unfair (and beside the point) to argue that since the various portraits did not look exactly the same that one of them must be wrong. As admirers of art, viewers would be disappointed if the various portraits *did* correspond too closely. Great art allows us to see the subject through an interpretation unique to the artist. The gospels of Mark and John certainly do that. Mark sees Jesus as a tragic figure, subject to the whims of cruelty, both willing and unwilling to die. John presents a heroic martyr that not only predetermines his own martyrdom but also transcends the suffering that accompanies it. Both portraits, nonetheless, are recognizable as Jesus. A literary appreciation of these gospels alongside one another forces the reader to view the character of Jesus as a multifaceted one. Looking closely, we can also find overlap between the two accounts. Although heroic in John, Jesus contains a small hint of the anxiety he reveals in Mark, when he admits his "soul is troubled." He represses this trouble very quickly, but it pops up ever so briefly to humanize Jesus very slightly. And even though Mark's Jesus wants to avoid death if he can, he also displays some Johannine heroic resignation in the statement "not my will but yours."

Viewing the gospels as adjacent literary interpretations eliminates the difficulty of contradictions within the gospels. New Testament readers often go down the blind alley of searching for the "real" Jesus, but the only remains of Jesus are literary portraits. As such, differences between the Jesuses should be no more bothersome than the conflicting actions and speeches of a character like Hamlet, who exemplifies both tenderness and callousness (toward Ophelia), both bravery and cowardice (with regard to revenge). What continues to intrigue readers of *Hamlet* is the contradiction embodied in Hamlet's character. Jesus would be much less fascinating were there fewer than four gospels, and his complexity diminishes greatly when one or more of them becomes subordinate to the others.

## Paul as interpreter of gospels

The canon of the New Testament presents the books anachronistically since Paul's letters predate the gospels. To read Paul in historical sequence would mean bracketing out any knowledge of the gospel accounts. In theory this seems easy since Paul betrays very little knowledge of the life of Jesus, but it proves difficult in actual practice because anyone who has even the most fleeting knowledge of the gospel stories tends to augment Paul's letters with the gospel stories. Paul talks about Jesus' crucifixion often but never mentions Pilate, Barabbas, Jesus' arrest, or the Garden of Gethsemane. As readers that have these events and people in our background knowledge, we inevitably think of the gospel narratives when reading Paul. If it were not for the gospels, Paul's many references to the crucifixion of Jesus would have almost no context. Within a canonical context, Paul's letters tend to be fleshed out, as it were, by the narratives of the gospels.

The interplay between Paul and the gospels works in the other direction as well. Surprisingly, the gospels give very little attention to the meaning of the crucifixion. Subtly, especially in John, a sacrificial death is hinted at, but none of the evangelists ponder greatly the question of why Jesus had to die; they mainly emphasize that it was necessary. It is not too much of an overstatement that they make a virtue of necessity. Paul, of course, sees the crucifixion as accomplishing a reconciliation between God and humanity. He calls the crucifixion an atonement for the sake of sin (Rom. 3:25). Given the extraordinary influence of Paul's interpretation, it is difficult to read the gospels without at least some of that influence coloring the significance of the events of the gospels.

Sometimes the differences between Paul's letters and the gospels have resulted in readers choosing between Jesus and Paul. When readers make this choice, they tend to describe Paul as one who distorts the message of Jesus. Two literary problems attach themselves to such a choice. First, to see Paul as one who twists Jesus' message assumes the objectivity of the gospels and overlooks the interpretive nature of those narratives. Second, it ignores the more pertinent question, "How does Paul's interpretation of the Jesus story expand our knowledge of the gospels?" Literarily, that question provides the greatest opportunity to read Paul vis-à-vis the gospels.

# The Book of Hebrews: Jesus as high priest

After Paul's letters comes the anonymous letter of Hebrews. Of all the books of the New Testament, Hebrews explains the most. By that, I mean that the author of this work considers it his task to present the significance of the figure of Jesus through means of a well-argued treatise. He does not concern himself with small details unless they fit into his cosmic argument about Jesus' significance. The author does not care for a conventional narrative of Jesus or even pieces of a conventional narrative. From Hebrews alone, the reader would know almost nothing about Jesus' life, except that he prayed and that he was crucified outside of Jerusalem; even Jesus' resurrection receives no mention. In an evocative metaphor, he dismisses the plain facts of Jesus' life as milk for children, and he assumes his audience should be gnawing on meat instead:

> Let us go on toward perfection, leaving behind the basic teaching about Christ, and not laying again the foundation: repentance from dead works and faith toward God, instruction about baptisms, laying on of hands, resurrection of the dead, and eternal judgment. (6:1–2)

Such a sentiment would be surprising to Mark or Paul, both of whom are quite concerned with the "basic teaching" of Christ and resurrection of the dead.

The author of Hebrews wants to move his listeners' attention from "what happened" to "what it means." In almost epic tones, this writer begins by placing the story of Jesus into the mythology of world history:

> Long ago God spoke to our ancestors in many and various ways by the prophets, but in these last days he has spoken to us by a Son, whom he appointed heir of all things, through whom he also created the worlds. He is the reflection of God's glory and the exact imprint

of God's very being, and he sustains all things by his powerful word. When he had made purification for sins, he sat down at the right hand of the Majesty on high, having become as much superior to angels as the name he has inherited is more excellent than theirs. (1:1–4)

This introduction tells the entirety of human history in a single Greek sentence. (The English translation breaks it into three sentences.) He thereby launches the most intellectually and rhetorically dazzling book of the New Testament. The treatise quotes from the Hebrew Bible dozens of times in order to show that Jesus has become both the new high priest and the final sacrifice, thereby abrogating the entire sacrificial system of Judaism. Although the author of Hebrews could not possibly have known his work would be included in the canon of the New Testament, this tract, by means of its confident vision, almost claims for itself preeminence. The forcefulness of his interpretations of the Hebrew scriptures, the certainty of his interpretation of Jesus, and the fierce warnings he directs toward those who might choose apostasy (see 6:4–8, 10:26–31, e.g.) do not invite debate.

The appearance of Hebrews within the canon presents yet one more interpretation of the Jesus story, one that has few commonalities with the rest of the canon. The image of Jesus as high priest belongs to this writer alone. Alongside Paul's letters and the gospel, Hebrews stands out like an aloof comrade, one that does not dialogue much with its partners but that is too formidable to ignore.

## The whole story

The canonical decisions that took place in the early church resulted in an act of surprising creativity. When the early Christians put together the canon, they formed a portrayal of Jesus that proved much more multifaceted than any of the individual books could have presented individually. Simultaneously the canon also invites and provokes the reader's creativity. The canon calls for readers willing to arrange the parts into a whole, to step back and envision a composite based on the individual pixels. Because we know that different authors composed them under various circumstances, we must also foster a kind of naïveté that allows for literary sensibilities to trump historical knowledge. Just as Paul uses the metaphor of the human body to describe the Corinthian church in 1 Corinthians, so also might the New Testament be seen as a body made of twenty-seven parts. Paul emphasizes that every person in the congregation has a specific function within the church body, urging the congregation to aim for interconnectedness rather than dissention. Literary appreciation of canon, using all twenty-seven pieces, also strives to find correlation.

At many stages in Christian history, readers have searched for a "canon within the canon" to smooth out the textual wrinkles of the New Testament. As a means of dealing with textual variety, interpreters sometimes opt for privileging one voice over another. Martin Luther famously described James as a "strawy" epistle since he saw James undermining the Pauline message of salvation by faith alone. For Luther, Paul's letters served as the canon within the canon, and he relegated James to a lesser status. What was at stake for Luther was theological doctrine. For other readers, the search for an interior canon stems from ethical concerns. Feminist readings often posit Galatians 3:28 as central ("in Christ there is ... neither male or female") and push more misogynistic texts to the margins.

From a literary standpoint, it makes little sense to speak of canon within a canon. All voices in the text must be allowed to speak; otherwise the reading fails. The ludicrousness of a canon within a canon comes into sharp focus by considering William Faulkner's *As I Lay Dying*, where fifteen different narrators contribute to the narrative of a family traveling to bury their matriarch. Not all of these narrators cohere with one another, but to take one voice as primary and to categorize the rest as secondary (or tertiary) does violence to the integrity of the novel. Of course, one might object that Faulkner's novel intentionally includes various points of view, and that his voice serves as the unifying hand for all these fictional characters. While recognizing the differences between the New Testament canon and Faulkner, such distinctions can be overstated. The unnamed organic creators of the biblical canon chose to canonize variety, just as Faulkner decided to embed it within a novel. Readers accustomed to thinking of God as the author of the New Testament differ little from those who see Faulkner as a unitary source. To put it bluntly, if both creators of canon and readers of it have been able to read the New Testament as a single work for hundreds of years, it remains a viable project. It may prove a daunting task—to hold plurality and singularity together is always difficult—but a literary reading of the whole opens up enormous possibilities for discovering the richness of the canonical decisions taken 1700 years ago.

# References

## Chapter 1

1. Augustine, *Confessions*, III. iv, trans. Henry Chadwick (Oxford: Oxford University Press, 1991), 40.

## Chapter 2

1. Kenneth Burke, "Literature as Equipment for Living," in *Contemporary Literary Criticism*, 2nd ed., ed. Robert Con Davis and Ronald Schleifer (New York: Longman, 1989), 81.

## Chapter 3

1. Some early manuscripts do not have this statement in the gospel. Even if it is not original, it certainly meshes with Luke's portrayal.

## Chapter 4

1. *The Antichrist*, trans. Walter Kaufmann, in *The Portable Nietzsche* (New York: Viking Press, 1968), 618.

## Chapter 5

1. D. H. Lawrence, *Apocalypse* (New York: Viking, 1932), 17–18.
2. Ibid., 22.

# Further reading

Alter, Robert, and Frank Kermode, eds. *The Literary Guide to the Bible*.
Cambridge: Harvard University Press, 1987.

Badiou, Alain. *St. Paul: The Foundation of Universalism*. Stanford:
Stanford University Press, 2003.

Barr, David L. *New Testament Story: An Introduction*. Belmont, CA:
Wadsworth, 2001.

——. *Tales of the End: A Narrative Commentary on the Book of
Revelation*. Santa Rosa, CA: Polebridge, 1998.

Besserman, Lawrence. *Chaucer's Biblical Poetics*. Norman: University
of Oklahoma Press, 1998.

Bible and Culture Collective. *The Postmodern Bible*. New Haven: Yale
University Press, 1995.

Castelli, Elizabeth. *Imitating Paul: A Discourse of Power*. Louisville:
Westminster/John Knox, 1991.

Crossan, John Dominic. *The Dark Interval: Towards a Theology of
Story*. Santa Rosa, CA: Polebridge, 1988.

Culpepper, Alan. *Anatomy of the Fourth Gospel: A Study in Literary
Design*. Philadelphia: Fortress, 1983.

Farrer, Austin. *A Rebirth of Images: The Making of St. John's
Apocalypse*. Albany: State University of New York Press, 1986.

Frei, Hans. *The Eclipse of Biblical Narrative: A Study in Eighteenth
and Nineteenth Century Hermeneutics*. New Haven: Yale
University Press, 1974.

Frye, Northrop. *The Great Code: The Bible and Literature*. New York:
Harcourt Brace Jovanovich, 1982.

——. *Words with Power: Being a Second Study of "The Bible and
Literature."* New York, Harcourt Brace Jovanovich, 1990.

Gabel, John B., Charles B. Wheeler, and Anthony D. York. *The Bible as Literature: An Introduction*. 4th ed. New York: Oxford University Press, 2000.

Jasper, David. *The New Testament and the Literary Imagination*. Atlantic Highlands, NJ: Humanities Press International, 1987.

Jeffrey, David Lyle. *People of the Book: Christian Identity and Literary Culture*. Grand Rapids, MI: Eerdmans, 1996.

Josipovici, Gabriel. *The Book of God: A Response to the Bible*. New Haven, Yale University Press, 1988.

Kermode, Frank. *The Genesis of Secrecy*. Cambridge: Harvard University Press, 1979.

Knox, John. *Chapters in a Life of Paul*. Rev. ed. Macon, GA: Mercer University Press, 1987.

Kort, Wesley. *Story, Text, and Scripture: Literary Interests in Biblical Narrative*. University Park: Pennsylvania State University Press, 1988.

Lienhard, Joseph. *The Bible, the Church, and Authority: The Canon of the Christian Bible in History and Theology*. Collegeville, MN: Liturgical Press, 1995.

Luz, Ulrich. *Studies in Matthew*. Trans. Rosemary Selle. Grand Rapids, MI: Eerdmans, 2005.

Metzger, Bruce. *The Canon of the New Testament: Its Origin, Development and Significance*. New York: Oxford University Press, 1987.

Miles, Jack. *Christ: A Crisis in the Life of God*. New York: Vintage, 2002.

Moore, Stephen. *Literary Criticism and the Gospels: The Theoretical Challenge*. New Haven: Yale University Press, 1989.

——. *Mark and Luke in Poststructuralist Perspectives: Jesus Begins to Write*. New Haven: Yale University Press, 1992.

Norton, David. *A History of the English Bible as Literature*. Cambridge: Cambridge University Press, 2000.

Prickett, Stephen. *Words and the Word: Language, Poetics and Biblical Interpretation*. Cambridge: Cambridge University Press, 1986.

Reed, Walter. *Dialogues of the Word: The Bible as Literature According to Bakhtin*. New York: Oxford University Press, 1993.

Resseguie, James. *Narrative Criticism of the New Testament: An Introduction*. Grand Rapids, MI: Baker Books, 2005.

Stendahl, Krister. *Paul among Jews and Gentiles and Other Essays*. Philadelphia: Fortress, 1976.

Stibbe, Mark W. G. *John as Storyteller: Narrative Criticism and the Fourth Gospel*. Cambridge: Cambridge University Press, 1995.

# Index

Index

Visit the
# VERY SHORT INTRODUCTIONS
Web Sites

# www.oup.com/uk/vsi
# www.oup.com/us

➤ **Information** about all published titles

➤ News of **forthcoming books**

➤ **Extracts** from the books, including titles not yet published

➤ **Reviews** and views

➤ **Links** to other **web sites** and main OUP web page

➤ Information about **VSIs in translation**

➤ **Contact** the editors

➤ **Order** other **VSIs** on-line

# Expand your collection of
# VERY SHORT INTRODUCTIONS

# THE OLD TESTAMENT
## A Very Short Introduction
Michael Coogan

Eminent biblical scholar Michael Coogan offers here a wide-ranging and stimulating exploration of the Old Testament, illuminating its importance as history, literature, and sacred text. Coogan highlights the significance of the history and literature of the Old Testament and describes how non-biblical evidence, such as archaeological data and texts, has placed the Old Testament in a larger and more illuminating context. He provides a marvelous overview of one of the great pillars of Western religion and culture, a book whose significance has endured for thousands of years and which remains vitally important today for Jews, Christians, and Muslims worldwide.

"By skillfully examining well-selected biblical texts, Coogan has offered readers a valuable window into the complexity, beauty, and importance of the Hebrew Bible...he clarifies the meaning of the Bible and allows the modern student to appreciate this complex ancient collection and its context."

**Marc Zvi Brettler, Dora Golding Professor of Biblical Studies, Brandeis University, author of *How to Read the Jewish Bible* and co-editor of *The Jewish Study Bible***

www.oup.com/uk/isbn/978-0-19-530505-0

# THE BIBLE
## A Very Short Introduction
John Riches

It is sometimes said that the Bible is one of the most unread books in the
world, yet it has been a major force in the development of Western culture
and continues to exert an enormous influence over many people's lives.
This Very Short Introduction looks at the importance accorded to the Bible
by different communities and cultures and attempts to explain why
it has generated such a rich variety of uses and interpretations. It explores
how the Bible was written, the development of the canon, the role of
Biblical criticism, the appropriation of the Bible in high and popular culture,
and its use for political ends.

> "Short in length, but not in substance, nor in interest.
> A fascinating introduction both to the way in which the Bible
> came to be what it is, and to what it means and has meant for
> believers. The examples are well-chosen and involving, and the
> discussion is erudite and original."
>
> **Joel Marcus, Boston University**

www.oup.com/uk/isbn/978-0-19-285343-1

# CHRISTIANITY
## A Very Short Introduction
Linda Woodhead

This Very Short Introduction offers a candid and wide-ranging overview of the world's largest religion. Linda Woodhead distinguishes three main types of Christianity—Church, Biblical, and Mystical—and examines their struggles with one another and with wider society.

Steering away from an idealistic approach, this introduction considers Christianity's relations with worldly power and its attempts to achieve social, political, economic and cultural dominance. It sheds light on Christianity's changing fortunes, and helps explain why a religion that is currently growing in much of the southern hemisphere is struggling to survive in parts of the West.

> "Faced with an almost impossible task of making a coherent and truthful selection of the emphases and themes, I don't think it could have been done better. Though very broad in its range, this is highly informed, observant and wise."
>
> **Iain Torrence, President, Princeton Theological Seminary**

www.oup.com/uk/isbn/978-0-19-280322-1